Especially for

_____

From

_____

Date

_____

POWER PRAYERS
for
Christmas

Marjorie
Vawter

BARBOUR BOOKS
An Imprint of Barbour Publishing, Inc.

© 2015 by Barbour Publishing, Inc.

Print ISBN 978-1-63409-202-9

eBook Editions:
Adobe Digital Edition (.epub) 978-1-63409-599-0
Kindle and MobiPocket Edition (.prc) 978-1-63409-600-3

Scripture quotations marked KJV are taken from the King James Version of the Bible.

Scripture quotations marked NIV are taken from the HOLY BIBLE, NEW INTERNATIONAL VERSION®. NIV®. Copyright © 1973, 1978, 1984, 2011 by Biblica, Inc.™ Used by permission. All rights reserved worldwide.

Scripture quotations marked MSG are from *THE MESSAGE.* Copyright © by Eugene H. Peterson 1993, 1994, 1995, 1996, 2000, 2001, 2002. Used by permission of NavPress Publishing Group.

Scripture quotations marked ESV are from The Holy Bible, English Standard Version®, copyright © 2001 by Crossway Bibles, a ministry of Good News Publishers. Used by permission. All rights reserved.

Scripture quotations marked NLT are taken from the *Holy Bible.* New Living Translation copyright© 1996, 2004, 2007, 2013 by Tyndale House Foundation. Used by permission of Tyndale House Publishers, Inc. Carol Stream, Illinois 60188. All rights reserved.

Scripture quotations marked NASB are taken from the New American Standard Bible, © 1960, 1962, 1963, 1968, 1971, 1972, 1973, 1975, 1977, 1995 by The Lockman Foundation. Used by permission.

Scripture quotations marked AMP are taken from the Amplified® Bible, © 1954, 1958, 1962, 1964, 1965, 1987 by The Lockman Foundation. Used by permission.

Published by Barbour Books, an imprint of Barbour Publishing, Inc., P.O. Box 719, Uhrichsville, Ohio 44683, www.barbourbooks.com

Our mission is to publish and distribute inspirational products offering exceptional value and biblical encouragement to the masses.

Member of the
Evangelical Christian
Publishers Association

Printed in the United States of America.

Contents

Introduction

Prayers are personal. No third party can ever express what's on your heart or write in your unique lingo or dialect, but when it seems like Christmas has turned into one giant to-do list or you find yourself forgetting the reason for the season, don't get discouraged—talk to your heavenly Father about it.

So find a semi quiet spot, push aside the sale ads and menu planning, and allow yourself to revel in the beauty, the bliss, and the blessings of this sacred season.

My Attitude

Paul wrote, "You must have the same attitude that Christ Jesus had" (Philippians 2:5 NLT). Jesus never held on to His deity as something that was His by right. Instead, He took on human form, grew up in the family the Father had carefully chosen, and never owned anything during His earthly ministry. Then, after three short years, He was arrested by the leaders of His own people and put to death on a cross—a cursed death, according to the Law. He didn't complain or refuse to do anything His Father asked Him to do. This is the attitude we desire.

Draw Near to God

Father, as we enter into this Christmas season, I desire to draw near to You. Quiet my spirit as I focus on the most precious gift of all—Your Son, born as a baby in a humble manger in a stable of Bethlehem, David's city. Born to die for my sin.

Guard your steps as you go to the house of God and draw near to listen rather than to offer the sacrifice of fools.
ECCLESIASTES 5:1 NASB

Renewal

Lord, so many times my attitude during the Christmas season is hard to keep right. It's so easy to forget the true meaning of the season in the hustle and bustle of parties, programs, shopping, and menu planning. May Your Holy Spirit renew my heart and mind as I make an attitude adjustment.

Instead, let the Spirit renew your thoughts and attitudes.
EPHESIANS 4:23 NLT

Pondering Hearts

When I ponder on the Christmas story, as Mary did, I want my heart attitude to be one of worship and wonder. You gave us an incredible gift when You sent Your Son to earth. Give me a heart of rejoicing like the shepherds had after seeing the child of whom the angels spoke.

The shepherders returned and let loose, glorifying and praising God for everything they had heard and seen.
LUKE 2:20 MSG

The "Perfect" Gift

Father, as the wise men brought gifts to Jesus, we give gifts at Christmastime. It's so easy to get caught up in finding the "perfect" gift or trying to outdo another on the extravagance of our gifts. Help me to remember that the only gift You desire is my heart surrendered to You.

The star. . .went ahead of [the wise men] and stopped over the place where the child was. . . . They entered the house. . .and they bowed down and worshiped him. Then they opened their treasure chests and gave him gifts of gold, frankincense, and myrrh.
MATTHEW 2:9, 11 NLT

A Servant's Heart

Mary had an attitude of humility and submission when she learned from the angel that she was to bear God's Son, the promised Messiah. Later she sang a song of praise to You, Lord. Help me to respond in the same manner to all You ask of me.

And Mary said, "Behold, the bondslave of the Lord; may it be done to me according to your word." And the angel departed from her.
LUKE 1:38 NASB

Joyful Obedience

Lord, in a day and a culture that killed women who bore children out of wedlock, Joseph can not be faulted for his initial hesitance to take Mary as his wife. But when the angel told him the truth about Mary, he immediately obeyed. Help me to respond to Your plans in the same way.

And Joseph awoke from his sleep and did as the angel of the Lord commanded him, and took Mary as his wife.
MATTHEW 1:24 NASB

Humility

Father, You didn't send Your Son as a king or a noble-man. He came to us as a baby to earthly parents of humble means, in order to experience human life from birth to death. Help me to strive to live with the attitude of humility He exhibited.

Have this attitude. . .which was also in Christ Jesus, who. . .
[took] the form of a bond-servant, . . .made in the likeness of men. . .
He humbled Himself by becoming obedient to the point of death.
PHILIPPIANS 2:5–8 NASB

Attitude Adjustment

Christ came to earth as a servant, and You ask us to live as He did. Help me to follow Jesus' example as I go about my everyday tasks during this busy season. And when I harbor a bad attitude, when things don't go my way, remind me that I need an attitude adjustment.

Let us therefore, as many as are perfect, have this attitude;
and if in anything you have a different attitude,
God will reveal that also to you.
PHILIPPIANS 3:15 NASB

Reflecting Christ

Father, I am so thankful You know me inside and out.
You know my thoughts, my desires, and my attitudes.
At this busy time of year, I want others to see Your Son's
humility and love shining through me. May my words
and actions be gracious and loving.

May the God who gives endurance and encouragement give you the
same attitude of mind toward each other that Christ Jesus had.
ROMANS 15:5 NIV

Christlikeness

Lord God, sometimes it's hard for me to respond in a
Christlike manner, especially when I'm surrounded by
people all looking out for themselves, not caring whom
they offend or hurt. Help me to be conscious of the
Spirit's presence within me, encouraging me to treat
others as Christ would.

If you serve Christ with this attitude,
you will please God, and others will approve of you, too.
ROMANS 14:18 NLT

A Godly Life

Lord God, You have not only given us the gift of salvation through Your Son, whose birth we celebrate at this time of year, but You have also told us how to live. Help me to live with an attitude of humility and kindness that reflects the character of Jesus Christ.

He has told you, O man, what is good;
and what does the LORD require of you but to do justice,
to love kindness, and to walk humbly with your God?
MICAH 6:8 NASB

God Knows Me

Lord, You know me through and through, better than I know myself. Each day I desire that You would search me, test my thoughts and attitudes about You, and lead me to make the changes that need to be made so that others will be drawn to You.

Yet you know me, LORD;
you see me and test my thoughts about you.
JEREMIAH 12:3 NIV

My Bible

The Bible is God's love letter to mankind. It is like
no other book ever written, nor ever will be. God
breathed His words into forty diverse human authors
over a 1,500-year period, resulting in sixty-six books.
The message is consistent throughout—there is one
true God and salvation is through Jesus Christ alone.
There are no contradictions or errors. God sends
His Word out, and it never returns to Him without
accomplishing His purposes. Be bold enough to believe
it, embrace it, devour it, breathe it, speak it, live it,
and love it. It is our milk, meat, and bread.

The Living Word of God

Lord, at this time of year, we celebrate the birth of Your Son. The Living Word became flesh. One hundred percent God, 100 percent man. Full of grace and truth, just as Your written Word is. May I be filled with Your presence this Christmas season.

And the Word became flesh, and dwelt among us. . .
full of grace and truth.
JOHN 1:14 NASB

Healing Word

Lord, so many in our world are hurting—physically, mentally, spiritually—bent on our own destruction. You predicted in Your written Word that You would send the Living Word to bring healing to Your troubled creation. We celebrate the fulfillment at Christmastime, and rejoice that we can be healed.

He sent His word and healed them,
and delivered them from their destructions.
PSALM 107:20 NASB

Sword of the Spirit

Father, You have given us special armor to wear in the constant battle with our enemy. Help me to learn to wield the sword of the Spirit—the Word of God—effectively. Help me to memorize the verses that will douse the fiery darts Satan hurls against me today.

Put on all of God's armor so that you will be able to stand firm against all strategies of the devil. . . . Put on salvation as your helmet, and take the sword of the Spirit, which is the word of God.
EPHESIANS 6:11, 17 NLT

Productive Word

Father, I'm so thankful that Your Word always accomplishes Your purposes. Just as the rain and snow water the earth and cause the seed to sprout and grow, so Your Word waters the hard soil of our hearts and bears the fruit You desire for each of us.

"The rain and snow come down from the heavens and stay on the ground to water the earth. They cause the grain to grow, producing seed for the farmer and bread for the hungry. It is the same with my word. I send it out, and it always produces fruit. It will accomplish all I want it to, and it will prosper everywhere I send it."
ISAIAH 55:10–11 NLT

Joyful Word

It is so easy to get caught up in the busyness of Christmas, Lord. We want to celebrate Your birthday with joy. Help me to protect the time I spend in Your Word, to not only read it but also to memorize and meditate on it day and night. ————————

But his delight is in the law of the LORD,
and in His law he meditates day and night.
PSALM 1:2 NASB

Success

Father, the world tells us that success is in the cars we drive or the jewelry we wear or the houses we live in. But You say that true success comes through studying and meditating on Your Word and then obeying the instructions and commands. Only this success lasts for eternity. ————————

"Study this Book of Instruction continually. Meditate on it day
and night so you will be sure to obey everything written in it.
Only then will you prosper and succeed in all you do."
JOSHUA 1:8 NLT

Saving Word

Father, it is through Your Word that I learn of my sin and my broken relationship with You. Because I delight in Your Word, I will not perish.

If Your law had not been my delight,
then I would have perished in my affliction.
PSALM 119:92 NASB

Doing His Will

Because Your living Word dwells within me, Father, it is a delight to do Your will. Help me to be a reflection of Your joy to a world lost in their sin.

"I delight to do Your will, O my God;
Your Law is within my heart."
PSALM 40:8 NASB

Diligent Study

Father, so many people have no clue as to the real reason for celebrating Christmas. I don't want to be ashamed of not knowing when I'm asked. Because of that, I desire to be a diligent student of Your Word, able to teach others the truth.

Be a good worker, one who does not need to be ashamed and who correctly explains the word of truth.
2 TIMOTHY 2:15 NLT

Prepared to Speak

Because I am Your child, Father, I need to be ready to "preach" Your Word, whether by my choices and actions or through interacting with others. With so many extra activities during the Christmas season, it's easy to be impatient and unloving. Help me to live Your Word daily.

Preach the word of God. Be prepared, whether the time is favorable or not. Patiently correct, rebuke, and encourage your people with good teaching.
2 TIMOTHY 4:2 NLT

Great Peace

Father, because I love Your Word, You envelop me with Your peace, which surpasses all comprehension. No matter what circumstances come against me, no matter what accusations the enemy brings against me, no matter if my family and friends turn against me, I will not stumble or fall.

Great peace have those who love your law,
and nothing can make them stumble.
PSALM 119:165 NIV

The Word of Christ

I love the music of the season, Lord, especially the old carols chock-full of the true story of Christmas. They speak to the Word of Christ indwelling me, and they encourage me to enter this busy time with joy and thanksgiving for the awesome gift of Your Son.

Let the word of Christ dwell in you richly, teaching and
admonishing one another in all wisdom, singing psalms and hymns
and spiritual songs, with thankfulness in your hearts to God.
COLOSSIANS 3:16 ESV

My Blessings

The apostle Peter wrote, "His divine power has granted to us all things that pertain to life and godliness, through the knowledge of him who called us to his own glory and excellence" (2 Peter 1:3 ESV). As we get to know Jesus Christ better, we learn to claim God's promises. We take delight in adding godly characteristics: moral excellence, knowledge, self-control, endurance, godliness, affection for others, and love. Out of these come God's richest blessings, abounding beyond our wildest imaginations. What better time than at Christmas should we count our blessings and name them one by one?

Covenant of Peace

Father, the birth of Your Son, Jesus Christ, over two
thousand years ago signaled the beginning of a new
covenant of everlasting peace with mankind. Unlike
the Law that was filled with judgment and punishment
for our inability to keep it, this new order came with
multiplied blessings, new every morning.

---

*I will make a covenant of peace with them; it shall be an everlasting
covenant with them, and I will give blessings to them and multiply
them and will set My sanctuary in the midst of them forevermore.*
EZEKIEL 37:26 AMP

Spiritual Blessings

How can I ever thank You enough, Father, for the blessings
that are mine because of Your Son? Your living Word
brings me *every* spiritual blessing possible. His birth proclaimed a new way of coming to You, restoring a relationship that had been broken by sin. Blessing upon blessing.

---

*Praise be to the God and Father of our Lord
Jesus Christ, who has blessed us in the heavenly
realms with every spiritual blessing in Christ.*
EPHESIANS 1:3 NIV

God's Sheep

Father, we celebrate the coming of Your Son to earth—
the Good Shepherd the psalmist king of Israel spoke of
so long ago. He knows His sheep, and His sheep know
Him. He provides eternal life, and He honors me with
overflowing blessings in the presence of my enemies.
How I praise You!

*You prepare a feast for me in the presence of my enemies. You honor
me by anointing my head with oil. My cup overflows with blessings.*
PSALM 23:5 NLT

Forgiven!

When I think that my sins—past, present, and future—
are forgiven, covered in the blood of Your Son, Father, I
know that I am truly blessed. Beyond what I could ever
imagine! You say that I am righteous, that there is no
deceit found in me. Mind-boggling, yet I am blessed!

*How blessed is he whose transgression is forgiven,
whose sin is covered! How blessed is the man to whom the LORD
does not impute iniquity, and in whose spirit there is no deceit!*
PSALM 32:1–2 NASB

Christmas Blessings

Father, the world's idea of Christmas blessings is solely based on material wealth, which leaves me out. Help me to remember that my worldly wealth means nothing to You. You have already given me the best gift ever—eternal life through the gift of Your Son.

"Test me in this and see if I don't open up heaven itself to you and pour out blessings beyond your wildest dreams."
MALACHI 3:10 MSG

Believing Faith

Oh, Father, please don't let me be a doubting Thomas, believing only that which I can see with my physical eyes. Give me the faith to believe that You will bless me beyond anything I can imagine in my wildest dreams. Give me twenty-twenty spiritual vision to see the better blessings this Christmas.

Jesus said, "So, you believe because you've seen with your own eyes. Even better blessings are in store for those who believe without seeing."
JOHN 20:29 MSG

Faithful God

Father, I praise You for Your faithfulness to me. Help me to wait on Your blessings instead of trying to provide for myself through my insignificant efforts.

So the LORD must wait for you to come to him so he can show you his love and compassion. For the LORD is a faithful God. Blessed are those who wait for his help.
ISAIAH 30:18 NLT

Distant Blessings

Father, this Christmas, help me to deal with my sin. I ask Your forgiveness for holding You and Your blessings at bay while I seek my own way.

"Your sins keep my blessings at a distance."
JEREMIAH 5:25 MSG

Freedom!

Father, You have rescued me from the enemy's slave market of sin through the gift of Your Son so many Christmases ago. You have set things right; You have released me from the power of sin. You have poured blessing upon blessing on me from Your protecting Rock.

Live, GOD! Blessings from my Rock, my free and freeing God,
towering! This God set things right for me and shut up the people
who talked back. He rescued me from enemy anger, he pulled me
from the grip of upstarts, He saved me from the bullies.
PSALM 18:46–48 MSG

Abundant Blessings

Oh, Lord! This Christmas I count the many blessings You have poured out on me, and I know that I truly am one of Your fortunate ones. I don't deserve anything from You, yet You have shown me the light and favor of Your love when You sent Your Son.

Blessed (happy, fortunate, to be envied) are the people who
know the joyful sound [who understand and appreciate
the spiritual blessings symbolized by the feasts]; they walk,
O Lord, in the light and favor of Your countenance!
PSALM 89:15 AMP

Giving Back

Lord God, You have given me so many blessings, I have no way of ever repaying You. But You remind me that Christmas is the perfect time to thank You in prayer and singing and to follow through on my promise of service to You for the ultimate gift of salvation.

What can I give back to GOD for the blessings he's poured out on me? I'll lift high the cup of salvation—a toast to GOD! I'll pray in the name of GOD; I'll complete what I promised GOD I'd do, and I'll do it together with his people.
PSALM 116:12–14 MSG

Invoke God's Blessings

Father, I am blessed to thank You and praise You for Your many blessings this Christmas. You have given me musical abilities to be used to lead others in worship and praise to You. I rejoice in the opportunities to proclaim the gift of Your Son to sinful people.

David appointed the following Levites to lead the people in worship before the Ark of the LORD—to invoke his blessings, to give thanks, and to praise the LORD, the God of Israel.
1 CHRONICLES 16:4 NLT

My Church

When Christ died, He abolished the system of the Law and temple worship. With His resurrection came a new order of doing things—the church. The apostles—including Paul, "the one born out of time"—established this new system of worship. Paul likened this new system to how a body works—many parts all working together for the good of one. Jesus is the head; believers make up the rest of His body. Each person receives at least one spiritual gift that he is to use to build up the body of believers.

Christ, the Head

Father, Your love for mankind sent Your Son into the world to conquer the sin problem. Then You established the church, with Christ our great High Priest as the head over the body. Help me to find my place in the overall body of believers, but specifically within my local body.

God has put all things under the authority of Christ and has made him head over all things for the benefit of the church. And the church is his body; it is made full and complete by Christ, who fills all things everywhere with himself.
EPHESIANS 1:22–23 NLT

Spiritual "Bullies"

Lord, You know that the "bullies" of this world would never be happy unless they were able to abuse someone. However, when the tables are turned and others pay back what they've been given, they are the first to yell, "Foul!" Help me to treat others as Christ treats us—with kindness.

No one abuses his own body, does he? No, he feeds and pampers it. That's how Christ treats us, the church, since we are part of his body.
EPHESIANS 5:29–30 MSG

Organized

You have established the church to do Your work now that
Christ has returned to You, Father. Christ organizes it and
puts believers into place so that each local congregation
can operate as an independent body. Help me to learn
what part You would have me play in my church.

*And when it comes to the church, he organizes
and holds it together, like a head does a body.*
COLOSSIANS 1:18 MSG

Speaking Truth

Father, I love my local church family. They are so
encouraging and loving. I truly see Jesus in them. We are
a small congregation, but Christ is definitely the head.
When rebuke or correction is in order, I know they have
prayed about it, and it will be done in love.

*Instead, we will speak the truth in love, growing in every way
more and more like Christ, who is the head of his body, the church.*
EPHESIANS 4:15 NLT

Part of the Whole

Lord God, the early church history fascinates me. Everyone had a part to play as they made up the body of Christ, just as each of us has a part today. Don't allow me to settle on a role that is not what You have called me to do.

You are Christ's body—that's who you are! You must never forget this. Only as you accept your part of that body does your "part" mean anything. . . . But it's obvious by now, isn't it, that Christ's church is a complete Body and not a gigantic, unidimensional Part?
1 CORINTHIANS 12:27, 29 MSG

Knowledge versus Love

Father, sometimes I fall into the trap of thinking I have more Bible knowledge than others in my church. But when I try to "share" it, people ignore me. Help me to remember that Your love when sharing my "knowledge" will make it much more acceptable. And may even close my mouth.

---

*We know that "we all have knowledge" about this issue.
But while knowledge makes us feel important,
it is love that strengthens the church.*
1 CORINTHIANS 8:1 NLT

Display God's Wisdom

Father, one of the reasons You established the church was so they could display to Satan and his hosts the truth of Christ's birth, death, and resurrection. How awesome!

God's purpose in all this was to use the church to
display his wisdom in its rich variety to all the unseen
rulers and authorities in the heavenly places.
EPHESIANS 3:10 NLT

Doing Good

Another way to show Your love and purpose in sending Jesus Christ to us, Father, is to love one another, doing good to everyone. Help me to be a good messenger of Your love.

Therefore, whenever we have the opportunity, we should do
good to everyone—especially to those in the family of faith.
GALATIANS 6:10 NLT

Guard God's People

Father, our example for living and ministering to unbelievers is Jesus Christ. He purchased the church with the shedding of His blood. Help me, especially at Christmastime, to put a hedge of Your protection around Your people. Give me the words to speak, the actions to take as I seek to live like Christ.

"So guard yourselves and God's people. Feed and shepherd God's flock—his church, purchased with his own blood—over which the Holy Spirit has appointed you as elders."
ACTS 20:28 NLT

Not a Stumbling Block

Father, I may understand what living in freedom means more than others within the church. But that still doesn't give me the right to do those things if they make anyone stumble and miss the path You have created specifically for each person.

Do not cause anyone to stumble, whether Jews, Greeks or the church of God.
1 CORINTHIANS 10:32 NIV

Gifts of the Spirit

Father, when You first established the church, the Holy Spirit took on a "new" position. Instead of indwelling select people for select purposes, the Spirit now indwells every believer. And then He distributes these gifts for the purpose of equipping God's people to do His work, building up the body of Christ.

Now these are the gifts Christ gave to the church: the apostles, the prophets, the evangelists, and the pastors and teachers. Their responsibility is to equip God's people to do his work and build up the church, the body of Christ.

EPHESIANS 4:11–12 NLT

Spotlessly Clean

Father, through Jesus' work on the cross, I have been washed by His cleansing blood and made holy and placed into His body, the church. I'm part of a vast number who have put their faith in Christ alone for salvation—pure, without spot or blemish, holy and without fault.

Christ loved the church. He gave up his life for her to make her holy and clean, washed by the cleansing of God's word. He did this to present her to himself as a glorious church without a spot or wrinkle or any other blemish. Instead, she will be holy and without fault.

EPHESIANS 5:25–27 NLT

My Family

Family. What a heartwarming word! At least in the way that God intended it. In the family unit, we learn to love each other, work through difficulties together, and build lasting relationships with one another. Then there's the family of God, those who are in the body of Christ.

For many people, the word *family* doesn't hold good memories. Maybe you're the only one left. That's where we learn that the body of believers is family, too. God places each person into families, so we never have to face life without earthly companions.

Dedicated to the Lord

Heavenly Father, I'm so thankful You put me into a family with godly parents, who early on dedicated me to You as Mary and Joseph did when they took Jesus to the temple. I ask that You would enable me to bless my children with the same godly heritage.

His parents took him to Jerusalem
to present him to the Lord.
LUKE 2:22 NLT

Family Joy

Lord God, marriage and family were the first institutions You established after You created the world and Adam and Eve. Ever since then You've cared for lonely souls by placing them in families—either traditionally or through Your church. Best of all, You have adopted us into Your family.

God places the lonely in families;
he sets the prisoners free and gives them joy.
PSALM 68:6 NLT

Cooperation

Father, I am blessed with the family You have given me here on earth—my parents, my siblings, my spouse, my children. You have used each one to teach me who I am and the purpose You have for me, not only here on earth but also within Your eternal family.

"You're blessed when you can show people how to cooperate instead of compete or fight. That's when you discover who you really are, and your place in God's family."
MATTHEW 5:9 MSG

Stick-to-itiveness

Father, Mary and Joseph gave us an example of how families stick together in trouble. When Joseph learned that Mary was with child before their marriage, he obeyed Your messenger and took her to be his wife contrary to the expectation of others. Help me to learn from their example when trouble visits my family.

Families stick together in all kinds of trouble.
PROVERBS 17:17 MSG

Problem Solving

Lord, You blessed Abraham when he chose not to fight with Lot over the land. He even gave Lot first choice as he honored Your plan for the family. Since I am part of Abraham's larger family of faith, give me grace to respond to family problems in like manner.

Abram said to Lot, "Let's not have fighting between us,
between your shepherds and my shepherds. After all, we're family.
Look around. Isn't there plenty of land out there? Let's separate.
If you go left, I'll go right; if you go right, I'll go left."
GENESIS 13:8–9 MSG

My Sister Wisdom

Father, in dealing with others, we need wisdom and insight. In fact, Your desire is that we consider these qualities as actual members of our families. Help me to see the value of treasuring these qualities as I do my sister or any other beloved family member.

Love wisdom like a sister; make insight
a beloved member of your family.
PROVERBS 7:4 NLT

Family Love

Heavenly Father, Paul's self-sacrificing attitude for his Messiah-rejecting family members is one I want to emulate. What an example of the love You have for me that caused You to send Your Son—the perfect God-man—to save me from my sin. Give me this kind of love for family members who reject You.

If there were any way I could be cursed by the Messiah so [the Israelites] could be blessed by him, I'd do it in a minute. They're my family.
ROMANS 9:3 MSG

Restoration

You have promised to restore all we sacrifice when we follow You, Lord. For many, the loss of family or homes is most keenly felt at Christmastime. Help me to be more sensitive to those who have suffered these losses, and to be the family they need all through the year.

"Anyone who sacrifices home, family, fields—whatever—because of me will get it all back a hundred times over, not to mention the considerable bonus of eternal life."
MATTHEW 19:29 MSG

Family Blessings

Father God, I rejoice in the family You have given me—earthly and spiritually. I rejoice in the restoration of some members who have chosen to go their own way in the past. And I rejoice in the additions to our family, growing us, restoring us, blessing us.

Oh, let GOD enlarge your families—giving growth to you, growth to your children. May you be blessed by GOD, by GOD, who made heaven and earth.
PSALM 115:14–15 MSG

Childless No More

Heavenly Father, thank You for the joy of parenthood. For those who are still waiting for that blessing, or for those whose children are already with You, Christmas can be difficult. Show me how I can be a blessing to others during this season and throughout the year.

He gives childless couples a family, gives them joy as the parents of children. Hallelujah!
PSALM 113:9 MSG

Accepted

Lord God, Jesus not only makes me holy, He accepts me into Your family as His sibling. What an amazing thought! That He could love a sinner such as I and become my righteousness is beyond my human comprehension. This Christmas, help me to proclaim this truth to those who don't know You.

Both the one who makes people holy and those who are made holy are of the same family. So Jesus is not ashamed to call them brothers and sisters.
HEBREWS 2:11 NIV

Beloved Family Member

Father, the gift of Your Son on that long-ago first Christmas brought us all into Your family. Jesus' birth, death, and resurrection transformed me from a stranger outside the family of faith into a beloved member of Your family. Jesus not only saved me from my sin, He also accepts me as a sibling.

So now you Gentiles are no longer strangers and foreigners. You are citizens along with all of God's holy people. You are members of God's family.
EPHESIANS 2:19 NLT

My Finances

Christmastime is an especially touchy time to talk about finances. Too many of us get caught up in the materialism of the season. Bank accounts get overdrawn, credit cards are "maxed out." Some people take out loans in order to have a "satisfactory" Christmas. But, in His Word, God has quite a bit to say about our finances, our money, and our investments. Moses, Solomon, Jesus, and Paul—they all dealt with this subject. In fact, it was one of Jesus' top subjects in His teaching. The Lord knows that where we spend our money is where our hearts are.

Give to Charity

Father God, I bring my finances before You. Since I can't take any money or possession with me when I die, I need Your perspective on how to spend what I earn. Jesus said to sell my possessions and give to those who need it. Help me to build my treasure in heaven.

"Sell your possessions and give to charity; make yourselves money belts which do not wear out, an unfailing treasure in heaven, where no thief comes near nor moth destroys. For where your treasure is, there your heart will be also."
LUKE 12:33–34 NASB

Treasure in Heaven

Lord, I want to build up my treasures in heaven where no thieves or moth or rust can steal or destroy them. Solomon said that if I have the means to help those in need, I must do it. Open my eyes to the needs of others whom I can help.

"Don't store up treasures here on earth, where moths eat them and rust destroys them, and where thieves break in and steal."
MATTHEW 6:19 NLT

The Root of All Evil

Father, too many times I've seen people grasp for money, work long hours, and still face financial ruin. They put their trust in money instead of You. Expose my love of money for what it is—sin. And forgive me when I cling to it more than I cling to You for provision.

But people who long to be rich fall into temptation and are trapped by many foolish and harmful desires that plunge them into ruin and destruction. For the love of money is the root of all kinds of evil. And some people, craving money, have wandered from the true faith and pierced themselves with many sorrows.
1 TIMOTHY 6:9–10 NLT

Never Enough

Pursuing the "almighty dollar" results in a sense of dissatisfaction. Money-loving people grasp at every opportunity to make more. . .and they are unhappy. Father, please keep me from falling into that trap. Help me to see that every paycheck is another opportunity to give back to You.

---

*Those who love money will never have enough.
How meaningless to think that wealth brings true happiness!*
ECCLESIASTES 5:10 NLT

Lending to God's People

Father, we've never had a lot of material goods or money, but on occasion we've had others ask us for a loan to get them through a rough patch. Some pay it back, but most have not, taking advantage of our policy of not charging interest. But You will make it right.

"If you lend money to any of my people who are in need, do not charge interest as a money lender would."
EXODUS 22:25 NLT

Be Generous

Lord, I believe that generosity and handling the money You give us is a sign of a believer with the right perspective. I want to be like those who are generous in lending money or meeting needs, even out of their own meager stores. That is true generosity.

Good comes to those who lend money generously and conduct their business fairly.
PSALM 112:5 NLT

Not Shaken

Father, those who handle their money according to the principles in Your Word don't falter when economic downturns destroy their investments. They can't be bribed. They can't be shaken. They know their "wealth" comes from You. Help me to learn from them, to imitate them, to trust You.

He does not put out his money at interest, nor does he take a bribe against the innocent. He who does these things will never be shaken.
PSALM 15:5 NASB

Two Masters?

Trying to serve two masters is exhausting and counter-productive. I know this, Father, but I still try to do it. When I serve the money god, it's very apparent I'm not trusting You. Money pulls me back into slavery. But I desire the freedom that trusting You brings. You are my master.

"No one can serve two masters. For you will hate one and love the other; you will be devoted to one and despise the other. You cannot serve both God and money."
MATTHEW 6:24 NLT

First-Day Offerings

Father, I'm thankful that You gave Paul insight as to how the church should take offerings. The requirements of a tithe in the Law were obsolete, but Paul encouraged believers to take a portion of their income and give it to You. Help me to follow the New Testament church example.

On the first day of every week, each one of you should set aside a sum of money in keeping with your income, saving it up, so that when I come no collections will have to be made.
1 CORINTHIANS 16:2 NIV

Lacking Nothing

When Jesus sent His disciples out to minister in the towns and villages, He sent them with only the bare necessities. In this way, they trusted the Lord to provide their needs: food, water, and shelter. Father, open my eyes to the needs of Your servants.

And He said to them, "When I sent you out without money belt and bag and sandals, you did not lack anything, did you?" They said, "No, nothing."
LUKE 22:35 NASB

Don't Be Dishonest

Father, it grieves me to hear of pastors who take off
with the church's money. They leave behind a devastated
church body struggling to overcome the dishonesty
of one who was supposed to be a wise manager. Help
me to discern when Your servants don't meet Your
qualifications.

---

*An elder is a manager of God's household, so he must live
a blameless life. He must not be. . .dishonest with money.*
TITUS 1:7 NLT

Be Content

Oh, Lord, learning to be content with what we have,
what You have given us, is hard. Paul said he was content
in every circumstance, whether in abundance or in lack.
You've been teaching me this lesson. Not easy, but I can
learn contentment because You strengthen me.

---

*Keep your lives free from the love of money
and be content with what you have.*
HEBREWS 13:5 NIV

My Friends

Friendships don't always come easily. God tells us about friendships like Jonathan and David had. Or as Moses had with God, standing face-to-face with one another, talking. The Lord challenges us to be a friend to others, using Himself as our example. Friends enrich our lives, praying for us, holding us up when we are weak. Friends not only love us in spite of ourselves, but they also challenge us to live in sold-out obedience to God.

Friendship with God

Father, You restored our ability to claim friendship with You when You planned for Your Son to take on Himself the sins of the world. As we celebrate His birth, we also celebrate our new relationship with You. We are no longer Your enemies because Jesus Christ came to earth.

For since our friendship with God was restored by the death of his Son while we were still his enemies, we will certainly be saved through the life of his Son. So now we can rejoice in our wonderful new relationship with God because our Lord Jesus Christ has made us friends of God.
ROMANS 5:10–11 NLT

Friends versus Slaves

Lord God, Jesus said that He no longer considers me a slave but a friend because He tells me all that the Father is doing. Because I worship You, I have the right to call You Friend. And You call me friend, just as You called Abraham, Moses, and Joshua friends.

God-friendship is for God-worshipers;
they are the ones he confides in.
PSALM 25:14 MSG

Face-to-Face

Father, You not only give me salvation, You also give me Your friendship. Scripture describes Moses as talking with You face-to-face as he did to his brother Aaron or his father-in-law Jethro. He considered both men friends. So today I can stand face-to-face in friendship with You because of Jesus Christ.

Inside the Tent of Meeting, the LORD would speak to Moses face to face, as one speaks to a friend.
EXODUS 33:11 NLT

Kindred Spirits

What a beautiful picture of friendship, Lord! From the moment they met, Jonathan and David were true "kindred spirits." It was a friendship that lasted long after Jonathan's death. I thank You for the friendships You have brought into my life, including the friendship I have with You through Jesus Christ.

By the time David had finished reporting to Saul, Jonathan was deeply impressed with David—an immediate bond was forged between them. He became totally committed to David. From that point on he would be David's number-one advocate and friend.
1 SAMUEL 18:1 MSG

Ultimate Friendship

Father, You showed the ultimate in friendship when You sent Your Son to die for my sin. Jesus willingly ransomed me from the slave market of sin so our friendship could be restored.

"Greater love has no one than this,
that one lay down his life for his friends."
JOHN 15:13 NASB

Sharpening Iron

Oh, Lord God, I am so thankful for the friendships You have given me. My friends don't hesitate to lovingly confront me when I am in the wrong.

As iron sharpens iron, so a friend sharpens a friend.
PROVERBS 27:17 NLT

Friend of Sinners

Father, You enabled the hymnist to write, "Jesus! what a Friend for sinners! Jesus! Lover of my soul." Friends on earth may fail me, but Jesus will not. Jesus called me His friend long before I was born. Accordingly, He keeps me up to date with what You are doing.

———————————

"I no longer call you slaves, because a master doesn't confide in his slaves. Now you are my friends, since I have told you everything the Father told me."
JOHN 15:15 NLT

Winning Friends

As the sowing and reaping principle plays out in every area of life, Lord Jesus, so it also works in friendship. A poet once wrote, "No man is an island." And how true that is. We need to be in relationship with others in order to flourish and to draw others to You.

———————————

The seeds of good deeds become a tree of life; a wise person wins friends.
PROVERBS 11:30 NLT

Fragrant Advice

Father, a popular gift at Christmas is perfume or cologne.
As these gifts give pleasure to my friends, help me to
take joy in their friendship. I can tell by the fragrance of
their words that they have spent time with You. Help me
to do the same for them.

Perfume and incense bring joy to the heart,
and the pleasantness of a friend springs from their heartfelt advice.
PROVERBS 27:9 NIV

A Kiss of Friendship

True honesty is as rare as the most precious jewel, Father.
But You have blessed me not only with Your friendship
through Jesus Christ's work on the cross, but also with
earthly friendships. Rare, precious jewels. A friend's
words are life giving and full of Your fragrance.

An honest answer is like a kiss of friendship.
PROVERBS 24:26 NLT

Loyal Friends

Lord, when life is going well, I can count my friends by the dozens. But when adversity comes, many who claimed to be my most loyal friends disappear. You have blessed me with a few friends who have stuck with me in the leanest times. That includes Your friendship.

Many will say they are loyal friends,
but who can find one who is truly reliable?
PROVERBS 20:6 NLT

Reliable Friendship

There have been a few times in my life when it seemed my friendships wouldn't hold up under the pressures of life, Father. But this Christmas, I rejoice that through it all I have a Friend in Jesus Christ, who never fails. He sticks with me through thick and thin.

One who has unreliable friends soon comes to ruin,
but there is a friend who sticks closer than a brother.
PROVERBS 18:24 NIV

My Gifts

One universally liked aspect of Christmas is gift giving. Likewise, the Holy Spirit gives gifts when we accept Christ as Savior. It's a fascinating study, and there are several "tests" or inventories we can take to discover what those gifts are. Some of the gifts are more prominent ones, like the gifts of teaching, preaching, and evangelism. Others can be worked out without drawing undue attention to oneself, like the gifts of helps, mercy, and administration. But the apostle Paul cautions believers not to work outside our gifting, because it usurps a spot the Lord intended for another and leads to discord in the church.

God's Indescribable Gift

Father, You gave the world the greatest of all gifts when You sent Your only Son to earth as a baby. His name is Jesus because He came to save His people from their sins. He is Immanuel, God with Us. Your Son is the reason we give gifts at Christmas.

Thanks be to God for His indescribable gift!
2 CORINTHIANS 9:15 NASB

Eternal Life

No one will ever give a gift like the one You give at salvation, Father God. The free gift of eternal life in Jesus Christ is ours when we believe by faith that He died on the cross and was raised from the grave, destroying the enemy's power over death and sin.

For the wages of sin is death, but the free gift
of God is eternal life in Christ Jesus our Lord.
ROMANS 6:23 NASB

Heaven's Gifts

Father of light, I know that every gift You give me is an outpouring of Your magnificent love—the same love that caused You to send Your Son that first Christmas. You have gifted me with so many things; my heart is in continual praise to You.

Every desirable and beneficial gift comes out of heaven.
The gifts are rivers of light cascading down from the
Father of Light. There is nothing deceitful in God,
nothing two-faced, nothing fickle.
JAMES 1:17 MSG

Diversity of Gifts

Lord, You delight in giving Your children gifts through Your Holy Spirit who dwells within each one of us. I'm very thankful that not only do You give me natural talents and abilities, but You also enhance many of those with the gifts of the Spirit. May I use them to bring You glory.

There are different kinds of gifts,
but the same Spirit distributes them.
1 CORINTHIANS 12:4 NIV

Proof of Salvation

Father, as I desire to give gifts to my children for Christmas and birthdays, so is Your desire. The gifts of Your Spirit are a seal—a proof—that I am truly Your child, adopted into Your family when I put my faith and trust in Jesus Christ alone for salvation.

*The unspiritual self, just as it is by nature, can't receive
the gifts of God's Spirit. There's no capacity for them.
They seem like so much silliness. Spirit can be known only by
spirit—God's Spirit and our spirits in open communion.*
1 CORINTHIANS 2:14 MSG

Appointed to Serve

Father, You give Your children gifts that will help others, especially within the church. Pastor; teacher; gifts of healing, helps, and administration—all benefit other believers, encouraging them to grow into maturity in Jesus Christ. Help me to discover my gifts and then rely on You for working them out.

*And God has appointed in the church, first apostles,
second prophets, third teachers, then miracles, then gifts of
healings, helps, administrations, various kinds of tongues.*
1 CORINTHIANS 12:28 NASB

Work to Excel

As I learn about the spiritual gifts You've given me, Lord God, help me to spend the necessary time to grow in them. While they benefit me and strengthen my walk with You, Your ultimate purpose in gifting me is to build up Christ's church, particularly my local assembly.

Since you are eager for gifts of the Spirit,
try to excel in those that build up the church.
1 CORINTHIANS 14:12 NIV

Serve One Another

Father, You have given to each believer at least one spiritual gift, to some more. Jesus said, "From everyone who has been given much, much will be required" (Luke 12:48 NASB). So help me to use the gifts You've given to serve other believers, in and out of my local church.

God has given each of you a gift from his great variety
of spiritual gifts. Use them well to serve one another.
1 PETER 4:10 NLT

Generous Gifting

Father, You have been generous with the gifts You've given me. With them, I desire to serve You, Your Son, and Your Spirit to encourage others to live for You, too.

May all the gifts and benefits that come from God our Father, and the Master, Jesus Christ, be yours.
1 CORINTHIANS 1:3 MSG

Be Bold

I know that You have not given me the spirit of fear, Father God. Help me to put away shyness and boldly serve You within the gifts You've given me.

God doesn't want us to be shy with his gifts, but bold and loving and sensible.
2 TIMOTHY 1:7 MSG

Confirmation

Father, I am filled with praise to You when You confirm the gifts of the Spirit in me. I feel Your joy and peace when I work within them, and they establish for me a place of ministry to others within the body of Christ.

But it is God Who confirms and makes us steadfast and establishes us [in joint fellowship] with you in Christ, and has consecrated and anointed us [enduing us with the gifts of the Holy Spirit].
2 CORINTHIANS 1:21 AMP

No Take-Backs

Lord God, You are the unchangeable God. You can never go back on Your Word. Nor can You lie. Therefore, when You give Your gifts—both spiritual and material—You can't withdraw them. When You call Your children to specific ministries, it also can't be taken back. Thank You for Your faithfulness.

For God's gifts and his call can never be withdrawn.
ROMANS 11:29 NLT

My Heavenly Father

God the Father appears in the Old Testament, but it wasn't until Jesus spoke of His intimate relationship with the Father that we saw that God wants to be our heavenly Father as well. Then the apostle Paul gives us more insight into this unique relationship between God and man. In Ephesians 1, he tells us that God chose to adopt us into His family before the foundation of the world. And in Romans 8, we're told that the Holy Spirit confirms the adoption when our spirits cry out, "Abba! Father!" What a joy to be an adopted son or daughter of God!

Begotten of the Father

Heavenly Father, on that long-ago first Christmas,
Your Living Word became flesh and lived as one of us for
thirty-three years. Jesus was 100 percent human. He told
His disciples that anyone who has seen Him has seen
You, for He was also 100 percent God. Amazing grace
and love divine.

And the Word became flesh, and dwelt among us,
and we saw His glory, glory as of the only begotten
from the Father, full of grace and truth.
JOHN 1:14 NASB

Perfect Father

Father, You are perfect, holy, beyond my human comprehension. Jesus, as the exact image of You in human form,
was perfect, without sin. Jesus told us that we are to be
perfect just as You are. The only way I can do that is to
live in Christ's righteousness.

"Therefore, you are to be perfect, as your heavenly Father is perfect."
MATTHEW 5:48 NASB

Daddy!

Father, when I put my faith in Christ for salvation, I was pretty young. You knew doubts might arise, but You placed Your Holy Spirit within me to confirm the reality of my salvation. At salvation You adopted me into Your family, and the Spirit responds when I call You *Abba*.

And because you are sons, God has sent the Spirit of his Son into our hearts, crying, "Abba! Father!"
GALATIANS 4:6 ESV

Perfect Gifts

It is so fun to pick out the "perfect" gifts for my children at Christmastime, Lord. How I love to watch their faces light up when I've gotten it right. You, my perfect heavenly Father, always get it right. Your gifts are so much more than I ask for.

"So if you sinful people know how to give good gifts to your children, how much more will your heavenly Father give good gifts to those who ask him."
MATTHEW 7:11 NLT

Family Member

Father, what a privilege it is to call You Father, just as the Lord Jesus does. The Spirit bears witness with my spirit when I meet other saints who are fellow citizens of heaven with me and who are members of Your household, my brothers and sisters in Christ. Thank You!

For through him we both have access in one Spirit to the Father.
So then you are no longer strangers and aliens, but you are fellow
citizens with the saints and members of the household of God.
EPHESIANS 2:18–19 ESV

Childlike Trust

This statement Jesus made, Father, comforts me. In answer to a question about who would be the greatest in His kingdom, Jesus called a child to Him and said, "No one can enter the kingdom without the trusting attitude of a child" (see Matthew 18). It is not Your will that anyone shall perish.

"It is not my heavenly Father's will that
even one of these little ones should perish."
MATTHEW 18:14 NLT

Perfect Parent

Father, You are the perfect parent—You have no favorites. Another way to say it is that You treat each one of Your children as Your favorite. Your blessings and judgments fall on each one in equal measure. I love coming into Your presence knowing that I have Your full attention.

And remember that the heavenly Father to whom you pray has no favorites. He will judge or reward you according to what you do. So you must live in reverent fear of him during your time here as "temporary residents."
1 PETER 1:17 NLT

A Father's Forgiveness

Heavenly Father, the majority of my prayers are full of asking for my own gain, rather than seeking forgiveness for my behavior toward others (or You). Even a prayer praising You is better than laying out my list like a child before Christmas. Examine my heart; remove the dross.

"And when you assume the posture of prayer, remember that it's not all asking. If you have anything against someone, forgive—only then will your heavenly Father be inclined to also wipe your slate clean of sins."
MARK 11:25 MSG

Obedience

Father, Jesus said that those who obey Your will are His true family. He was making the distinction between His earthly half brothers who did not believe He was Your Son at that time. You have adopted me into Your family. May I obey Your will, so others will know to whom I belong.

[Jesus] stretched out his hand toward his disciples.
"Look closely. These are my mother and brothers.
Obedience is thicker than blood. The person who obeys my
heavenly Father's will is my brother and sister and mother."
MATTHEW 12:49–50 MSG

I'm Adopted!

Lord, I love to meet people who have adopted or are adopted, to hear their stories of how they were especially chosen by their adoptive parents. You chose me specifically, too. Long before the foundation of the world. What a wonderful privilege it is to call You "Abba, Father."

But you have received the Spirit of adoption
as sons, by whom we cry, "Abba! Father!"
ROMANS 8:15 ESV

A Father's Provision

Father, You take Your role of my heavenly Father seriously, and You provide all I need. Jesus spoke often of Your provision for all creation, including the birds. They don't sow and reap, but they never go hungry. I know I am more valuable than they are, and You will provide for me.

"Look at the birds of the air; they do not sow or reap or store away in barns, and yet your heavenly Father feeds them. Are you not much more valuable than they?"
MATTHEW 6:26 NIV

No Worries

Lord, worry over where the money will come from to pay for food, clothing, and shelter dominates the minds of those who don't know You. Too often I catch myself worrying over these things. Please remind me of Your faithfulness to provide for Your children.

"These things dominate the thoughts of unbelievers, but your heavenly Father already knows all your needs."
MATTHEW 6:32 NLT

My Home

God designed the home and family back in the Garden of Eden. Since that time He has made provision for establishing homes and families. Solomon had a lot to say about the home in Proverbs: a wise woman builds up her home, but a foolish woman tears it down; through godly wisdom a home is established; God puts children into homes He designed for them. Then there are the scriptures that describe godly homes versus the homes of the wicked. Finally, Jesus said He was returning to the Father's house to prepare places for us in our eternal home—heaven.

Builder Wisdom

Father, I want to provide a godly home for my children and grandchildren. But I know from reading Your Word that I need to have Your wisdom to establish my home on a sound and good foundation. One way I can do this is by telling my children about Jesus' birth at Christmas.

*Through skillful and godly Wisdom is a house
(a life, a home, a family) built, and by understanding
it is established [on a sound and good foundation].*
PROVERBS 24:3 AMP

A Blameless Life

Another way to establish a godly home, Lord God, is to live blamelessly and with integrity before my family. It certainly isn't anything I can do on my own, for I must strive to live a life that reflects Your Son's. And for that, I need Your help and wisdom.

*I will be careful to live a blameless life—when will you come
to help me? I will lead a life of integrity in my own home.*
PSALM 101:2 NLT

Wise Woman/Foolish Woman

Lord God, I believe one of the reasons You chose Mary to be Jesus' mother was because of her wisdom, knowing she would provide the right atmosphere for Him to flourish.

A wise woman builds her home, but a foolish woman tears it down with her own hands.
PROVERBS 14:1 NLT

Prosperous Homes

Father, You delight in prospering godly homes with godly wives who bear strong, godly children. What a joy it is to watch children grow strong in You.

Your wife will be like a fruitful grapevine, flourishing within your home. Your children will be like vigorous young olive trees as they sit around your table.
PSALM 128:3 NLT

Hospitality

Lord, one of the qualifications of a pastor is the gift of
hospitality. I thank You for those who open their homes
to guests, especially at Christmastime, when many are
lonely.

*An elder. . .must enjoy having guests in his home,
and. . .must live wisely and be just.*
TITUS 1:7–8 NLT

Learning to Share

Christmas is an especially difficult time for those who
struggle financially to provide meals and a warm home
for their families. Father, help me to meet these needs for
someone this year.

*Cheerfully share your home with those
who need a meal or a place to stay.*
1 PETER 4:9 NLT

Salvation and Rejoicing

Father, thank You for the promises in Your Word, especially for those who establish their homes on You. In these homes children grow up seeing Your strong right hand of power at work. You bring salvation through Your Son, and with that comes rejoicing, especially at Christmas when we celebrate Christ's advent.

The voice of rejoicing and salvation is in the tents and
private dwellings of the [uncompromisingly] righteous:
the right hand of the Lord does valiantly and achieves strength!
PSALM 118:15 AMP

Godliness at Home

Father, Mary's godly life, even as a young girl, was why You chose her as the mother of Your Son. Later, Paul writes to Timothy about the importance of mothers of all ages to live godly lives first in their homes. As a result, many go on to love and serve You.

Their first responsibility is
to show godliness at home.
1 TIMOTHY 5:4 NLT

Our Eternal Home

Our eternal home is with You, Father. And You consider Yourself at home among Your people, those who love and serve You. Jesus said He was going to prepare an eternal home for us. For this reason, we say that those who die in You have gone to their true home.

I heard a loud shout from the throne, saying, "Look, God's home is now among his people! He will live with them, and they will be his people. God himself will be with them."
REVELATION 21:3 NLT

Plague-Free Homes

Oh, Father, how often I have prayed for Your protection over my earthly home, over my children and their families. In return You promise shelter and refuge from the evil one. Even when we don't have much in the material sense, You provide as You did for Mary and Joseph at Jesus' birth.

If you make the LORD your refuge, if you make the Most High your shelter, no evil will conquer you; no plague will come near your home. For he will order his angels to protect you wherever you go.
PSALM 91:9–11 NLT

Heavenly Home

What a wonderful promise Jesus gave us, Father. In preparing His disciples for His death, resurrection, and return to Your house, He told them that He was going to prepare dwelling places for them and for all who trust Him for salvation, just as You provided a home for His earthly life.

"In My Father's house are many dwelling places; if it were not so, I would have told you; for I go to prepare a place for you."
JOHN 14:2 NASB

At Home with Jesus

Father, what a great comfort to know that when I die, I am instantly home with You and Jesus in heaven—my eternal home. From scripture we know this world isn't our home. Believers don't really fit in here. But while we are here, we point others to Christ.

We are of good courage. . .and prefer rather to be absent from the body and to be at home with the Lord.
2 CORINTHIANS 5:8 NASB

My Hope

The writer of Hebrews gave us the definition of the
believer's hope: "Faith is the confidence that what we
hope for will actually happen; it gives us assurance about
things we cannot see" (11:1 NLT). The believer's hope
is eternal salvation in heaven with the Savior of our
souls. This isn't an "Oh I wish" kind of hope; this is an
absolute certainty that something we haven't seen yet
will be reality one day. Without hope, we are miserable
people with nothing to live for; with hope, we have all of
eternity's wonders and realities in which to rejoice.

A Good Future

Father, just as You encouraged the Jews in captivity in Babylon, so You also encourage me today. Such a wonderful promise! You have good plans for me. Plans that give me hope for a good and fulfilling future. Things might look grim right now, but remembering the Christmas story renews my hope.

"'For I know the plans I have for you,'
declares the LORD, 'plans for welfare and not
for calamity to give you a future and a hope.'"
JEREMIAH 29:11 NASB

My Hope Is in the Lord

Father, thank You for the hope I find in You. As I do battle with the enemy of my soul who would love to steal my joy, You hear my cries for help and remind me that Jesus came so that I might have a never-ending hope in You.

We put our hope in the LORD.
He is our help and our shield.
PSALM 33:20 NLT

Never Disappointed

"My hope is in the Lord, who gave Himself for me."
Father God, the words to that old hymn speak of the
reasons why I can put my complete trust in Jesus Christ.
Because He is my hope, I can never be put to shame or
be disappointed in You.

O my God, I trust, lean on, rely on, and am confident in You.
Let me not be put to shame or [my hope in You] be disappointed;
let not my enemies triumph over me. Yes, let none who trust and
wait hopefully and look for You be put to shame or be disappointed.
PSALM 25:2–3 AMP

Joyful Hope

Father, I don't know how people live without hope.
When Jesus was born, hope took on flesh. Hope is
eternal, it is my anchor, and it encourages me to walk
forward in obedient faith in You. Each day the promise
of hope—heaven—is closer and more real. Thank You.

Be joyful in hope, patient in affliction, faithful in prayer.
ROMANS 12:12 NIV

Courageous Hope

Oh, Father, some days I need more courage and strength than others just to get out of bed and face the day ahead. Knowing that my hope in You is sure and steadfast, the anchor that keeps me from drifting too far, helps me keep my eyes on You.

"Having hope will give you courage.
You will be protected and will rest in safety."
JOB 11:18 NLT

Confident Hope

Father, I don't have the gift of being able to see what will happen in the future. But I do know that Your plans for me give me hope to keep moving forward. It's not an "I wish" type of hope but a confidence that what You have promised You are able to perform.

Faith is the confidence that what we hope for will actually happen;
it gives us assurance about things we cannot see.
HEBREWS 11:1 NLT

Hope in God

When I put my hope in You, Father, You have promised to provide for me and see the wicked destroyed. The wicked are not trustworthy. I must hope in You alone.

Put your hope in the LORD. Travel steadily along
his path. He will honor you by giving you
the land. You will see the wicked destroyed.
PSALM 37:34 NLT

Hope in God's Love

Lord God, I have put my hope in You, largely due to the overwhelming awe Your unfailing love inspires in me. In fact, scripture says that You delight in those who do put their hope in You.

The LORD delights in those who fear him,
who put their hope in his unfailing love.
PSALM 147:11 NIV

Hope's Focus

Lord God, You promise to wrap me in Your perfect and constant peace when I keep my focus on You. For You are an everlasting Rock. You never change. Therefore, I can confidently put my hope and trust in You alone. Your peace shields me from the world and the enemy's fiery darts.

You will guard him and keep him in perfect and constant peace whose mind [both its inclination and its character] is stayed on You, because he commits himself to You, leans on You, and hopes confidently in You. So trust in the Lord (commit yourself to Him, lean on Him, hope confidently in Him) forever; for the Lord God is an everlasting Rock.
ISAIAH 26:3–4 AMP

Hope against Hope

Father, all who come to You in faith, believing in Christ alone for salvation, are Abraham's spiritual children. He hoped in—believed—Your promise to make his and Sarah's descendants as numerous as the stars, even when there was no basis because of their ages. Increase my faith; restore my hope today.

Even when there was no reason for hope,
Abraham kept hoping—believing.
ROMANS 4:18 NLT

Glorious Hope

Lord, the believer's glorious hope is the surety of eternal salvation through faith in Jesus' work on the cross. So give me the boldness to speak of my salvation and testify of my Savior. The worst that can happen is that I might be martyred for my faith—and be with You eternally.

*Since we have such [glorious] hope (such joyful and confident
expectation), we speak very freely and openly and fearlessly.*
2 CORINTHIANS 3:12 AMP

Enduring Hope

Father, I want to be known for my enduring hope in You. Often we see the word *hope* in Christmas cards, on Christmas coffee mugs, and other places. That's because when Jesus was born, the surety of hope dawned in mankind's hearts. My hope is in Jesus Christ alone!

*As we pray to our God and Father about you,
we think of your faithful work, your loving deeds,
and the enduring hope you have because of our Lord Jesus Christ.*
1 THESSALONIANS 1:3 NLT

My Joy

"The joy of the LORD is your strength," Nehemiah told
the Jews returning from exile in Babylon (Nehemiah
8:10 NIV). With all the tricks of the enemy against them,
they were getting discouraged at the monumental task
of rebuilding the temple and Jerusalem. Today, the
truth of Nehemiah's statement is still true. Joy is a river
running deep in our souls, bubbling up on occasion to
burst out in unparalleled rejoicing. Even in the most
difficult times, joy is a constant spring underneath
the enemy's scorched-earth tactics.

Tidings of Joy

As the God of hope, Father, You fill me with joy. Each
Christmas I read the story of how Jesus was born of the
virgin Mary, and how the joy of knowing that God had
come to earth resulted in great joy, spoken by the angel
and reflected in the star.

Now may the God of hope fill you with all joy and peace in believing,
so that you will abound in hope by the power of the Holy Spirit.
ROMANS 15:13 NASB

Refuge Joys

Lord God, You are good! In You I take refuge from the
storms of life, from the fierce battles with the enemy, and
from the stressors of a busy life. Your joy fills me with
the same joy the shepherds and wise men experienced so
long ago.

Taste and see that the LORD is good.
Oh, the joys of those who take refuge in him!
PSALM 34:8 NLT

Joyful Singing

Lord God, because of Jesus, joy bubbles out of my spirit like a spring that never goes dry. Even when life is difficult and dark, joy underlies everything like a deep underground pool—all because of Your salvation by faith alone in Christ Jesus. I sing for joy, for You are my Refuge.

But as for me, I shall sing of Your strength; yes, I shall joyfully sing of Your lovingkindness in the morning, for You have been my stronghold and a refuge in the day of my distress.
PSALM 59:16 NASB

Complete Joy

Father, Jesus spoke on many topics while in the upper room with His disciples the night He was arrested. In spite of what He knew would happen in the next few days, He wanted them—and us—to know joy that is only complete when we abide in Him.

"I have told you this so that my joy may be in you and that your joy may be complete."
JOHN 15:11 NIV

Joy in Trials

Even in the middle of deep trials, Father, I have Your joy bubbling up like a spring. And You say there's even more joy ahead, when we see Christ face-to-face. Though I have never seen Him, I shall know Him by the print of the nails in His hand.

So be truly glad. There is wonderful joy ahead, even though you must endure many trials for a little while. . . . You love him even though you have never seen him. Though you do not see him now, you trust him; and you rejoice with a glorious, inexpressible joy.
1 PETER 1:6, 8 NLT

Joy in Jesus' Glory

Father, it seems crazy to rejoice in suffering. . .until I understand Your purpose for trials. They make me a partner with Christ's sufferings. Trials refine me, pull the dross out, and reveal Jesus' glory. One day soon, I shall be like Him. How can I help but rejoice?

Instead, be very glad—for these trials make you partners with Christ in his suffering, so that you will have the wonderful joy of seeing his glory when it is revealed to all the world.
1 PETER 4:13 NLT

Choose Joy

Father, I confess it's difficult to find joy in the trials You allow in my life, until I look at Jesus. Certainly there was joy at His birth and resurrection. But joy in His suffering and death? Yes. He endured it all, despising the shame, for the joy set before Him.

Consider it all joy, my brethren,
when you encounter various trials.
JAMES 1:2 NASB

Joyful Mimics

I am to imitate the attitudes of Your Son and of believers who have gone before me, Father. They show me how to have joy in spite of severe suffering. Only those who have Your Spirit living within them know the unfathomable depths of joy that permeate a persecuted believer.

You became imitators of us and of the Lord,
for you welcomed the message in the midst of severe
suffering with the joy given by the Holy Spirit.
1 THESSALONIANS 1:6 NIV

Future Joy

In spite of the prospect of extreme suffering and a cruel death, Father, from which Jesus in His humanity shrank, He looked beyond the grave to the joy You set before Him. Joy made Him able to go through death to the resurrection in order to save me from my sin.

Fixing our eyes on Jesus. . .who for the joy set
before Him endured the cross, despising the shame,
and has sat down at the right hand of the throne of God.
HEBREWS 12:2 NASB

Like-Minded Joy

Father, Paul's letter to the Philippians is a refreshing discourse on how to have Your joy in spite of circumstances and people. Imprisoned in Rome for the sake of the Gospel, he urged them to live in one spirit and mind and love. Keep my focus on Jesus, as Paul did.

Make my joy complete by being like-minded,
having the same love, being one in spirit and of one mind.
PHILIPPIANS 2:2 NIV

Fruit of the Spirit

Father, joy is another theme of Christmas. The angel told the shepherds that he had tidings of great joy for them. Joy is also a part of the fruit of the Spirit that You develop in Your children when they trust Jesus alone for salvation. Joy permeates the very bedrock of my faith.

But the fruit of the Spirit is love, joy, peace,
patience, kindness, goodness, faithfulness.
GALATIANS 5:22 NASB

Full Measure of Joy

Lord, whenever I read through Jesus' prayer during His last "upper room" time with His disciples, I am in awe. He prayed for *me* that night. He knew He was facing the suffering and shame of the cross, but He wanted me to know the fullness of joy found only in Him.

"I am coming to you now, but I say these things
while I am still in the world, so that they may
have the full measure of my joy within them."
JOHN 17:13 NIV

My Needs

We are a needy people, no matter where we fall on the income ladder. God created us with certain basic needs for life: food, water, shelter, love. One need, though, that many go through life without even being aware it's a need is the problem of our sin nature. A theme in scripture is how God has made provision for all our needs, including the sin problem. All we have to do is ask Him. . .and then wait on Him for the answer.

Needs Satisfied

Father, You delight to meet the needs of Your children.
Like the three Hebrew men who refused to bow to
Nebuchadnezzar's image and were cast into the fiery
furnace but did not die or even receive scorch marks, so
You satisfy my desires in the sun-scorched times of life.

---

*"The LORD will guide you always; he will satisfy your needs in a
sun-scorched land and will strengthen your frame. You will be like
a well-watered garden, like a spring whose waters never fail."*
ISAIAH 58:11 NIV

Provision for Needs

How often have I claimed this promise, Lord God! And
how often You prove Your faithfulness in keeping Your
promises. Because of the materialism that has hijacked
the Christmas season, I tend to think that my "wants" are
needs, too. Help me to keep the right perspective this year.

---

*And my God will supply all your needs according
to His riches in glory in Christ Jesus.*
PHILIPPIANS 4:19 NASB

Our Needs Are Known

Father, You know my needs even before I do. Remind me of this whenever I'm tempted to worry about not having new clothes or food to satisfy my hunger or money to meet the basic necessities of life. Those without Christ worry because they don't know how You provide for Your children.

"These things dominate the thoughts of unbelievers all over the world, but your Father already knows your needs."
LUKE 12:30 NLT

All Needs Met

Lord God, You have promised to answer before I even know I have a need. Even when I know the need, I tend to talk about it—and worry about it—before I bring it to You. Help me to be more aware of Your answers to my unspoken prayers.

"I will answer them before they even call to me. While they are still talking about their needs, I will go ahead and answer their prayers!"
ISAIAH 65:24 NLT

Just Enough

Father, true satisfaction is found in Jesus' shed blood spilled for my sin. Spiritual satisfaction runs over into my daily life where I desire just enough to fulfill my needs. I don't want to be rich or in poverty, for both bring dissatisfaction. Give me enough to satisfy my needs.

Give me neither poverty nor riches!
Give me just enough to satisfy my needs.
PROVERBS 30:8 NLT

Devoted to Doing Good

Lord, Your definition of productiveness and mine often-times differ. Jesus said He did all the Father asked Him to do. He provided for the most urgent needs and didn't allow Himself to be distracted by what wasn't on Your agenda. In the same way, help me to be productive.

Our people must learn to devote themselves to doing what is good,
in order to provide for urgent needs and not live unproductive lives.
TITUS 3:14 NIV

Need for Forgiveness

Father, above all other needs mankind has is the need for forgiveness. Even above the necessities of life—food and water, shelter, money enough to provide those—is the need to deal with the heavy burden of sin. You are the One who made the way. I praise You for forgiving me.

But there is forgiveness with You [just what man needs],
that You may be reverently feared and worshiped.
PSALM 130:4 AMP

Urgent Needs

Lord, the prophet Micah told us Your requirements for doing good: do justly, love kindness, and walk humbly with You. When I do good, I am living in a blameless, productive way. I am able to provide the basic needs of life (and more) to my family and to others.

And what does the Lord require of you? To act justly
and to love mercy and to walk humbly with your God.
MICAH 6:8 NIV

Build Others Up

Father, many of the people You bring across my path
are so needy. Not necessarily in the material, but in the
spiritual and emotional sense. But so many times I let
words flow from my mouth without a filter. Instead of
building them up, I do damage. Guard my tongue today.

Do not let any unwholesome talk come out of your mouths,
but only what is helpful for building others up according
to their needs, that it may benefit those who listen.
EPHESIANS 4:29 NIV

Trust God

Lord, I love that not only do You provide for our basic
needs of life, but You also give us everything we need
for our enjoyment. You know that we need our hobbies
or fun times with family and friends in order to be fully
equipped to face the difficult times.

Teach those who are rich in this world not to be proud and not to
trust in their money, which is so unreliable. Their trust should
be in God, who richly gives us all we need for our enjoyment.
1 TIMOTHY 6:17 NLT

Supply the Needs of Believers

Father, when I work within Your purpose, I provide a
service that meets the specific needs of Your people.
Sometimes that is through giving either monetarily or
providing a meal for a family that is struggling. When
I teach Your Word, You use me to meet spiritual needs.
Thank You.

*This service that you perform is not only supplying
the needs of the Lord's people but is also overflowing
in many expressions of thanks to God.*
2 CORINTHIANS 9:12 NIV

Help in Time of Need

Lord, I am blessed beyond measure with friends who
pray for me and stick loyally by me when others turn
away. I am even more blessed in my family, my siblings,
my spouse, my children. They circle round whenever one
of us is in need. My cup overflows.

*A friend is always loyal, and a brother
is born to help in time of need.*
PROVERBS 17:17 NLT

My Patience

Patience. We know we need it. But we also know that the best way to learn it is through difficult circumstances when we must wait, wait, and wait some more before getting any answers. Have you ever noticed the ones who don't fidget or fuss in the waiting area when a flight has been delayed or a doctor has had an emergency to deal with? Those are the ones who have been in a similar situation many times before, and they know there's nothing to be gained by fussing. Let's see what God has to say.

Fruit of Patience

Father, it takes a lot of patience to get through the Christmas season in this crazy world. Tempers flare up over trivial matters, crowds populate every arena of life, and false "reasons for the season" abound. This year I want all the fruit of the Spirit to overflow. Yes, even patience.

But the fruit of the Spirit is love, joy, peace,
patience, kindness, goodness, faithfulness.
GALATIANS 5:22 NASB

Strengthened with Patience

Father God, we often joke about praying for patience because it usually means You provide more opportunities to exercise this virtue. The apostle Paul knew that patience is impossible to achieve without Your power. So the next time I need patience, help me to remember to pray for Your supernatural power.

We also pray that you will be strengthened with all his glorious
power so you will have all the endurance and patience you need.
COLOSSIANS 1:11 NLT

Steadfast Patience

Father, this faith life isn't easy. You tell us that Jesus knows this from experience. It's what makes Him the perfect High Priest. Help me to call on Him for the patience and endurance I need to accomplish Your will and receive and enjoy the fruit of Your promises.

For you have need of steadfast patience and endurance,
so that you may perform and fully accomplish the will
of God, and thus receive and carry away [and enjoy
to the full] what is promised.
HEBREWS 10:36 AMP

Filled with Patience

Several times in scripture, Lord, You talk about the importance of patience and self-control in living the life You have called me to. As I grow older in years, I should also mature in my faith so that I can teach those who are younger than I how to live.

Teach the older men to exercise self-control, to be worthy
of respect, and to live wisely. They must have sound
faith and be filled with love and patience.
TITUS 2:2 NLT

Full Results of Patience

Father, one of the purposes of trials is that they produce patience and endurance. You allow the trials to prove my faith. Because of the difficult times of these last months or years, I have developed patience waiting on You to perfect and mature me. Thank You for continually guiding me.

Be assured and understand that the trial and proving of
your faith bring out endurance and steadfastness and patience.
But let endurance and steadfastness and patience have full play
and do a thorough work, so that you may be [people] perfectly
and fully developed [with no defects], lacking in nothing.
JAMES 1:3–4 AMP

Patience Better Than Pride

Lord, I have several unfinished projects around the house. Most of them were fun to start, but then the tediousness set in and I finally set them aside to start something else. I lack the patience to endure to the end. Give me the stick-to-itiveness to complete all You give me to do.

Finishing is better than starting. Patience is better than pride.
ECCLESIASTES 7:8 NLT

Passionate Patience

Father, Your Word says to rejoice in trouble when it comes, especially when trouble seems to multiply like rabbits. The apostle Paul said that "passionate patience" results from the difficult times of life. I want this patience—enduring, sustaining, and persevering. A patience that "forges the tempered steel of virtue."

We continue to shout our praise even when we're hemmed in with troubles, because we know how troubles can develop passionate patience in us, and how that patience in turn forges the tempered steel of virtue.
ROMANS 5:3–4 MSG

Prove Yourselves

Father, if my actions speak louder than my words, then my walk must imitate You. Exhibiting Your patience is difficult for me. You waited until "the fullness of time" (Galatians 4:4 ESV) had come before sending Jesus to redeem mankind. I need Your patience as I pray for unbelieving friends and family members.

We prove ourselves by our purity, our understanding, our patience, our kindness, by the Holy Spirit within us, and by our sincere love.
2 CORINTHIANS 6:6 NLT

A Heart of Patience

Lord, Your Word says that one of the signs that I have been chosen of You is a heart of patience, along with several other qualities. Patience is a virtue that I—by nature—don't have. Patience has to be developed by the Spirit over time. Along with the Spirit's other fruit.

So, as those who have been chosen of God, holy and beloved,
put on a heart of compassion, kindness, humility,
gentleness and patience.
COLOSSIANS 3:12 NASB

Perfect Patience

Father, Your Spirit works in me, molding me into the image of Your Son. It takes time, contrary to most things we want in today's expectation of instantaneous gratification. In Your Word, You have included examples of godly people who have persevered in their spiritual walk. I want to follow in their steps.

But I obtained mercy for the reason that in me, as the foremost
[of sinners], Jesus Christ might show forth and display all His perfect
long-suffering and patience for an example to [encourage] those who
would thereafter believe on Him for [the gaining of] eternal life.
1 TIMOTHY 1:16 AMP

Wait with Patience

The hope I cling to is the culmination of my salvation, Lord, the knowledge that one day I will be in heaven with You for eternity. Then the reality of living in Your presence will make the hardships of this world worth it all. For this I can wait with patience.

But if we hope for what is still unseen by us,
we wait for it with patience and composure.
ROMANS 8:25 AMP

Patience of Christ

Lord God, You faithfully direct my path and protect me from the machinations of the enemy. Direct my way into Your amazing and incomprehensible love, and develop patience in me as I wait for Christ's return—the same patience that characterized His walk on earth.

May the Lord direct your hearts into [realizing and showing]
the love of God and into the steadfastness and patience
of Christ and in waiting for His return.
2 THESSALONIANS 3:5 AMP

My Peace

Over the ages, peace has been an elusive commodity. Instead, war and bickering and arguments with our neighbors or in our families or politically or between religions takes precedence. When the angel announced Jesus' birth to the shepherds, the angelic host joined him, proclaiming, "Glory to God in highest heaven, and peace on earth to those with whom God is pleased" (Luke 2:14 NLT). One of Jesus' names is Prince of Peace. Lasting peace is only found in Jesus Christ.

Peace on Earth

Father, You chose to announce the birth of Your Son to shepherds tending their sheep. They were terrified when they saw the angel herald. But the angel proclaimed the arrival of the Prince of Peace and gave glory to You for fulfilling Your promise made to Isaiah.

"Glory to God in the highest heaven,
and on earth peace to those on whom his favor rests."
LUKE 2:14 NIV

Peace in Heaven

Over two thousand years ago, the eternal King of kings was born in a stable, into a humble family. Isaiah prophesied many names for this baby, all indicative of His deity, and all bringing glory to You, Father God. The divine peace of heaven came to earth that night.

"Blessings on the King who comes in the name of the LORD!
Peace in heaven, and glory in highest heaven!"
LUKE 19:38 NLT

Peace in Christ

Father, peace is a precious commodity in our world. Even those who search for it rarely find it, for without Jesus, peace is elusive. But Jesus has overcome all the world's false beliefs. And those who truly seek Him will find the peace that surpasses all understanding.

"These things I have spoken to you, so that in Me you may have peace. In the world you have tribulation, but take courage; I have overcome the world."
JOHN 16:33 NASB

Let Peace Rule

Since peace is so rare though mankind strives so hard to find it, Father God, Your peace seems unrealistic. As Your child, I am called to peace. But worry and the cares of this world choke it out. Help me to let it rule my heart and my actions.

Let the peace of Christ rule in your hearts, since as members of one body you were called to peace.
COLOSSIANS 3:15 NIV

Peaceable Wisdom

Lord, James describes Your wisdom with several qualities I desire to have, such as purity, mercy, reasonableness, and being without hypocrisy. But the quality of peace permeates them all. As I make choices to walk in Jesus' footsteps each day, envelop me with Your peace that surpasses all understanding.

But the wisdom from above is first pure, then peaceable,
gentle, reasonable, full of mercy and good fruits,
unwavering, without hypocrisy.
JAMES 3:17 NASB

Lord of Peace

Father, one of Jesus' names is Prince of Peace. He never was hurried, though His public ministry was only three short years. He never rushed through a teaching moment, though people with urgent needs called out to pull Him away. Surround me with His peace no matter the circumstances.

Now may the Lord of peace Himself continually
grant you peace in every circumstance.
2 THESSALONIANS 3:16 NASB

Live Peacefully

Father, today we hear so much about war, nations that refuse to make peace with other nations. Even the world You sent Jesus into wasn't peaceful. The Romans held a tentative peace in the lands they conquered. In the midst of unrest today, my desire is to live quietly and peacefully.

Make it your ambition and definitely endeavor to live quietly and peacefully, to mind your own affairs, and to work with your hands, as we charged you.
1 Thessalonians 4:11 AMP

At Peace

Father, when Jesus came the first time, He brought peace to those who believed in Him. He told His disciples that He was leaving peace with them, freed of their fears, when He returned to heaven. And when He comes again, He wants His church to be at peace still.

Be eager to be found by Him [at His coming] without spot or blemish and at peace [in serene confidence, free from fears and agitating passions and moral conflicts].
2 Peter 3:14 AMP

Work for Peace

Father, if Your peace isn't in my heart, I can't be at peace with others. So fill me with the satisfaction and contentment that comes from living like Christ.

---

*"God blesses those who work for peace,
for they will be called the children of God."*
MATTHEW 5:9 NLT

Life and Peace

Father, at times my thoughts swirl in my mind until I am exhausted, and they still don't settle. They rob me of sleep and peace, and I start to slip into the pit of despair. But when I let Your Spirit take them captive, I experience the peace I desperately need.

---

*So letting your sinful nature control your mind leads to death.
But letting the Spirit control your mind leads to life and peace.*
ROMANS 8:6 NLT

God's Unsurpassing Peace

"Peace, peace, wonderful peace, coming down from the Father above!" I desire Your peace, Father. When I give my worries to You by praying about them and thanking You for the reminder to pray, I feel Your peace surrounding me. My thoughts quit clamoring for attention in my mind, and I rest.

Don't worry about anything; instead, pray about everything. Tell God what you need, and thank him for all he has done. Then you will experience God's peace, which exceeds anything we can understand. His peace will guard your hearts and minds as you live in Christ Jesus.
PHILIPPIANS 4:6–7 NLT

Live in Peace

The apostle Paul told us that as much as it is possible, we are to live in peace with one another, Lord. This is the peace we find through the Prince of Peace.

God has called us to live in peace.
1 CORINTHIANS 7:15 NIV

My Praise

"Man's chief end is to glorify God and to enjoy Him forever." The *Westminster Shorter Catechism* begins with this statement. God created man to glorify Him, to praise Him. Down through the ages we've found the easiest way to praise Him is through song. David, the sweet psalmist of Israel, comes to mind. Paul tells the churches in Ephesus and Colosse to sing "psalms, hymns, and spiritual songs" in order to encourage one another and to bring praise to God into their services.

Worthy of Praise

Father, I love the songs of Christmas, especially those that proclaim praise to You for sending Your Son to be the perfect sacrifice for the sins of mankind. Jesus is the spotless Lamb of God who alone is worthy to receive all my praise. "Worthy is the Lamb."

"Worthy is the Lamb, who was slain, to receive power and wealth and wisdom and strength and honor and glory and praise!"
REVELATION 5:12 NIV

The Sacrifice of Praise

Because Jesus was the perfect Lamb of God offered up for my sin, I desire that my life be a continual sacrifice of praise to You, Father. Eternity in heaven will be a constant carol of praise from all the redeemed, one which the angels cannot sing.

Through Him then, let us continually offer up a sacrifice of praise to God, that is, the fruit of lips that give thanks to His name.
HEBREWS 13:15 NASB

Praise His Name

Father, You are my God. Even before the foundation of the world You chose me to be Your child. You planned out each detail of my life so that I accomplish Your purpose. I can't help but praise You when I see Your plans come to fruition.

O Lord, I will honor and praise your name, for you are my God.
You do such wonderful things! You planned them long ago,
and now you have accomplished them.
ISAIAH 25:1 NLT

Wonderfully Made

Oh, Lord, when I think about how I am made, how all the little parts and pieces of my body work together in wonderful synchronicity, I am amazed. You plan everything down to the tiniest detail. What an awesome and amazing God! I can never cease to praise You.

I praise you because I am fearfully and wonderfully made;
your works are wonderful, I know that full well.
PSALM 139:14 NIV

Eternal Praise

Lord, how I love to sing Your praise! You who are so worthy of all praise. Sometimes I wonder what it will be like in heaven—an eternity to praise You.

Open my lips, Lord,
and my mouth will declare your praise.
PSALM 51:15 NIV

Thankful Praise

Father, I have so many loved ones who have gone on before me and entered the gates of heaven with thanksgiving and praise on their lips. Soon I'll join them.

Enter His gates with thanksgiving and His courts
with praise. Give thanks to Him, bless His name.
PSALM 100:4 NASB

Praise the Savior

Father, since You are my heavenly Father, You want my life in Christ to be one long peal of praise. As the hymnist wrote two centuries ago, "Praise the Savior, ye who know Him! Who can tell how much we owe Him? Gladly let us render to Him all we are and have."

And whatever you do [no matter what it is] in word or deed, do everything in the name of the Lord Jesus and in [dependence upon] His Person, giving praise to God the Father through Him.
COLOSSIANS 3:17 AMP

Praise Music

Lord God, almost since the beginning of time You have given man the ability to make music, to praise You with voices and instruments. Paul gave instructions to the fledgling church about offering praise. No wonder music is a major part of my worship in my quiet times with You.

Speak out to one another in psalms and hymns and spiritual songs, offering praise with voices [and instruments] and making melody with all your heart to the Lord.
EPHESIANS 5:19 AMP

Worthy of Praise

Father, when I allow my thoughts to run wild with little or no effort to control them, I find myself slipping into depression. You gave us a list of the kinds of thoughts that are pleasing to You: if anything is worthy of praise—Jesus Christ—think on Him.

Finally, brethren, whatever is true, whatever is honorable,
whatever is right, whatever is pure, whatever is lovely,
whatever is of good repute, if there is any excellence and
if anything worthy of praise, dwell on these things.
PHILIPPIANS 4:8 NASB

A Chosen People

Father, You chose me before the foundation of the world to serve You, to be one of Your special possessions. The thought boggles the human mind to think that Your love for me reaches back that long ago. All I can do is praise You for calling me into Your light.

But you are a chosen people, a royal priesthood, a holy nation,
God's special possession, that you may declare the praises of
him who called you out of darkness into his wonderful light.
1 PETER 2:9 NIV

For the Praise of His Glory

Father, the apostle Paul told the Ephesian church that You chose each believer to live for the praise of Your glory. So when I put my trust in Jesus Christ for salvation, I fulfilled this primary purpose of mankind—to glorify You. Make my life one of joyful praise to You.

We who first hoped in Christ [who first put our confidence in Him have been destined and appointed to] live for the praise of His glory!
EPHESIANS 1:12 AMP

A New Song

Father God, You fill my mouth with songs of praise. You have delivered me in so many ways—from the penalty and power of sin, from depression that at times threatens to overwhelm me, from the enemy's attacks. Give me boldness to sing Your praise that others might trust in You.

He put a new song in my mouth, a song of praise to our God; many will see and fear and will trust in the LORD.
PSALM 40:3 NASB

My Savior

The angel came to Joseph one night to reassure him that
Mary hadn't been unfaithful. She'd been chosen to give
birth to God's Son. Joseph was given the name for the
baby: Jesus, for He would save His people from their sin.
Jesus fulfilled every prophecy in the Old Testament.
He was the promised Messiah, the Savior, the onetime
perfect sacrifice only the perfect High Priest could make for
a believer's atonement. Jesus' death, burial, and resurrection
paid sin's penalty and freed the believer from the power of
sin. One day our salvation will be complete when we enter
heaven's gates and leave sin's presence behind.

Call Him Jesus

Father, Jesus was born to die. Your angel told Mary and Joseph, individually, to name the Son of God at His birth. You chose this name because of its meaning.

"And you shall call his name Jesus,
for he will save his people from their sins."
MATTHEW 1:21 ESV

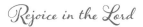

Rejoice in the Lord

No matter what happens, Lord, I will rejoice in You, for You are my Savior. My job and source of income may disappear, food may be scarce and expensive because of natural disasters, and I could lose my home and possessions. But who else on earth or in heaven do I need but You?

Though the fig tree does not bud and there are no grapes on the vines,
though the olive crop fails and the fields produce no food, though
there are no sheep in the pen and no cattle in the stalls, yet I will
rejoice in the LORD, I will be joyful in God my Savior.
HABAKKUK 3:17–18 NIV

My Savior

Father God, because You sent Your Son to die as the perfect sacrifice for my sin, the enemy of my soul is defeated. But he still accuses me in an attempt to keep me defeated. However, You not only are my Savior, You are also my Refuge, Shield, and Deliverer.

"The LORD is my rock and my fortress and my deliverer; my God, my rock, in whom I take refuge, my shield and the horn of my salvation, my stronghold and my refuge; my savior, You save me from violence."
2 SAMUEL 22:2–3 NASB

Rejoice in the Savior

Mary's example of immediate submission to Your will, Father, resulted in this song of praise. As one of Your redeemed ones, may I be just as quick to praise You.

"My soul glorifies the Lord and my spirit rejoices in God my Savior."
LUKE 1:46–47 NIV

Saved to Be Holy

Father, You saved me and called me to a holy life in the Savior, Jesus Christ. You chose me before the beginning of time to receive this gift. When He came to earth as a baby, You sent Him full of grace and truth, to teach us of You and Your salvation.

He has saved us and called us to a holy life—not because of anything we have done but because of his own purpose and grace. This grace was given us in Christ Jesus before the beginning of time, but it has now been revealed through the appearing of our Savior, Christ Jesus.
2 TIMOTHY 1:9–10 NIV

My Redeemer King

Isaiah prophesied so long ago about Your role as my Savior and Redeemer, Lord Jesus. But not all the world accepts that yet. One day every knee will bow and every tongue will confess that You are King of kings and Lord of lords, but above all, the Savior of the world.

"All the world will know that I, the LORD, am your Savior and your Redeemer, the Mighty One of Israel."
ISAIAH 49:26 NLT

The Right Time

Father, at that first Christmas when Your Son, Jesus, was born into the world, You "announced" Your plan of salvation—a plan that has been in place since before the foundation of the world. And ever since, You have entrusted Your children with the work of telling our peers about it.

And now at just the right time [God] has revealed this message, which we announce to everyone. It is by the command of God our Savior that I have been entrusted with this work for him.
TITUS 1:3 NLT

Savior of the World

Father, You sent Your Son to be the Savior of the world. Your plan for getting the word out to all people and all nations is for all who have trusted Him for salvation to testify to those who haven't heard. Help me to fulfill my part in Your plan.

Furthermore, we have seen with our own eyes and now testify that the Father sent his Son to be the Savior of the world.
1 JOHN 4:14 NLT

Salvation of Hope

Because of Jesus' birth, life, death on the cross, and resurrection, Lord, I have hope founded in You alone. That's why Christmas is a high point for me. Jesus was born to die. . .for *my* sin.

This is why we work hard and continue to struggle,
for our hope is in the living God, who is the Savior
of all people and particularly of all believers.
1 TIMOTHY 4:10 NLT

Mighty Savior

Lord God, You are the mighty Savior. When You set Your plan in motion so long ago, You decided to live among the people You created, taking on flesh. Because I am Yours, You calm my fears with Your love. You rejoice over me with joyful songs. You take delight in me.

"For the LORD your God is living among you. He is a mighty savior.
He will take delight in you with gladness. With his love, he will
calm all your fears. He will rejoice over you with joyful songs."
ZEPHANIAH 3:17 NLT

Mary's Praise Song

Mary sang Your praises after You chose her to be Your Son's mother, Lord. She knew He was the mighty Savior because of the name You gave Him—Jesus, for He shall save His people from their sins. Open my mouth to sing praise to my Redeemer, my Savior.

"Praise the Lord, the God of Israel, because he has visited and redeemed his people. He has sent us a mighty Savior from the royal line of his servant David."
LUKE 1:68–69 NLT

The Return of the Savior

Father, one of the Christmas carols we sing—"Joy to the World"—not only speaks of Christ's first coming as a baby but also of His second coming. Both times He comes as my Savior—first from the penalty and power of sin and second from the presence of sin.

But we are citizens of heaven, where the Lord Jesus Christ lives. And we are eagerly waiting for him to return as our Savior.
PHILIPPIANS 3:20 NLT

My Thanks

The songwriter says to "count your blessings, see what God has done." The fact is, the blessings are innumerable and our resulting thanks are infinite.

God has indeed done marvelous things, and He is deserving of all the thank-yous His people can give Him. One way to counteract discouragement, depression, and lack of motivation is to start writing down everything we have to be thankful for. And start saying "Thank You" out loud. God has done marvelous things. Give thanks always, for all things.

God's Indescribable Gift

Father, it is hard to put into words the enormity of the gift of Your Son to a lost, sinful, and dying world. Yet, when the time was just right, You sent the Savior, the One whose sacrifice paid our sin debt. For that alone, I am eternally grateful.

Thanks be unto God for his unspeakable gift.
2 CORINTHIANS 9:15 KJV

Victory

For the victory through Jesus Christ over sin and death, I thank You, Father. For the ability to stand firm in the face of "impossible" situations, I thank You. For knowing that the work You have called me to do in Jesus is not full of empty results, I thank You.

But thanks be to God! He gives us the victory through our Lord Jesus Christ. Therefore, my dear brothers and sisters, stand firm. Let nothing move you. Always give yourselves fully to the work of the Lord, because you know that your labor in the Lord is not in vain.
1 CORINTHIANS 15:57–58 NIV

The Fruit of Our Lips

Father, Christmas is a time to thank You once again for the gift of salvation You gave the world when You sent Jesus. Because of Him, I will continually offer a sacrifice of praise to You. My tongue cannot be silent, for I can't help but sing Your praise.

Through Him then, let us continually offer up a sacrifice of praise to God, that is, the fruit of lips that give thanks to His name.
HEBREWS 13:15 NASB

Shout for Joy

Lord God, every year I am thankful that our "holy days" begin with Thanksgiving in November. From there it is easy to continue to enter Your presence with thankfulness in the following weeks leading up to Christmas. Because of Your gift of a Savior, I have much for which to thank You.

O come, let us sing for joy to the LORD, let us shout joyfully to the rock of our salvation. Let us come before His presence with thanksgiving, let us shout joyfully to Him with psalms. For the LORD is a great God and a great King above all gods.
PSALM 95:1–3 NASB

A Song of Thanksgiving

Father, a line in one of the gospel songs we sing says, "Count your many blessings, name them one by one." This may be an endless task, because there is so much for which to thank You. You are my Strength and Shield. And that's just the beginning. Thank You!

The LORD is my strength and my shield; my heart
trusts in Him, and I am helped; therefore my
heart exults, and with my song I shall thank Him.
PSALM 28:7 NASB

Mourning into Dancing

Sometimes the darkness seems to stretch endlessly before me, Lord. But You have promised to turn my mourning into dancing. I know You have already done this for me in other circumstances. So my soul can only say thanks and my voice sings Your praise. I cannot be silent.

You have turned for me my mourning into dancing;
You have loosed my sackcloth and girded me with gladness,
that my soul may sing praise to You and not be silent.
O LORD my God, I will give thanks to You forever.
PSALM 30:11–12 NASB

Overflow with Thankfulness

Father, in the Old Testament, the growing believer's faith is likened to a tree planted near a water source. Paul carries this theme into the New Testament when he encourages us to put down deep roots anchored in and built on Jesus. As my faith grows stronger, my heart truly overflows with gratefulness.

Let your roots grow down into him, and let your lives be built on him. Then your faith will grow strong in the truth you were taught, and you will overflow with thankfulness.
COLOSSIANS 2:7 NLT

God's Will

There are times when I've found it difficult to thank You for my circumstances, Lord. But Your will is for me to express my gratitude for *all* that happens. *All* is a small word that encompasses absolutely everything. This is Your will. When I am obedient, I find I am truly thankful.

Be thankful in all circumstances, for this is God's will for you who belong to Christ Jesus.
1 THESSALONIANS 5:18 NLT

Jesus Gives Thanks

Your ways are not our ways, Father. So I don't always understand why You chose me, one who is foolish and "not quite right in the head," according to the wisdom of the world. But Jesus said that You make known Your ways and plans to those whom the world laughs at. Thank You.

Jesus rejoiced, exuberant in the Holy Spirit. "I thank you, Father, Master of heaven and earth, that you hid these things from the know-it-alls and showed them to these innocent newcomers. Yes, Father, it pleased you to do it this way."
LUKE 10:21 MSG

Give Thanks, for He Is Good

Lord, I have so much to thank You for, especially at Christmas. I suppose it's because I'm more focused on Jesus, the One who became flesh and lived on earth. Because of His sacrifice, He is my eternal High Priest, good and faithful in all things. What wondrous love, steadfast and eternal.

Oh give thanks to the LORD, for he is good; for his steadfast love endures forever!
1 CHRONICLES 16:34 ESV

Thanksgiving Gate

Father, when I think of who You are, I can't stop thanking You or singing Your praises for choosing me and adopting me into Your family. You are good. You love me with an everlasting love. Your faithfulness is for all generations. "Praise God from whom all blessings flow."

Enter his gates with thanksgiving, and his courts with praise!
Give thanks to him; bless his name! For the LORD is good;
his steadfast love endures forever, and his faithfulness
to all generations.
PSALM 100:4–5 ESV

Wonderfully Made

Father, when I think of the complexity of the human body and know that You created it, I am in awe. Everything You programmed into my DNA is exactly what I need to live a life of purpose and praise to You. Thank You, "for I am fearfully and wonderfully made."

I will give thanks to You, for I am fearfully and wonderfully made;
wonderful are Your works, and my soul knows it very well.
PSALM 139:14 NASB

My Time

Because God is eternal and ageless, He isn't bound by
time. In fact, He created time—day and night. Yet we
are told that when the time was exactly right, He sent
Jesus into the world. Today is the day of salvation. Our
days are numbered. So we see that He allows Himself
to work within time parameters we understand. We
talk about God's timetable for events that have already
happened or will happen soon, but in reality we're the
ones who need the timetable. One day we'll be
in eternity where time no longer matters.

Number Your Days

Time is such a precious commodity here on earth, Father, but not one by which You are bound. I am one who works best with a list, knocking off each task as it's completed. But I still waste a lot of time. Forgive me. May Moses' prayer be mine this Christmas.

So teach us to number our days
that we may get a heart of wisdom.
PSALM 90:12 ESV

My Days Are Numbered

Father, I don't know the number of years You've allotted for me here on earth. But no matter how long my life is, it will be brief. Remind me of this when I am pressed for time. Each moment counts when we remember how fleeting life is.

"LORD, remind me how brief my time on earth will be.
Remind me that my days are numbered—how fleeting my life is."
PSALM 39:4 NLT

No Shortcuts

Father, at times I'm overwhelmed with all the time-saving tools available to make me "successful." But Your Word says that there are no shortcuts to make me successful in Your eyes. That is only found in the time I spend in Your Word, meditating on it throughout each day.

"Don't look for shortcuts to God. The market is flooded with surefire, easygoing formulas for a successful life that can be practiced in your spare time. Don't fall for that stuff, even though crowds of people do. The way to life—to God!—is vigorous and requires total attention."
MATTHEW 7:13–14 MSG

Wasting Time

Lord, Christmas is such a busy time, it's easy for me to consider time spent in Your Word as a waste of time. But You say that the true waste of time is in not doing what You command me to do—like sharing the true meaning of Christmas with others.

Merely hearing God's law is a waste of your time if you don't do what he commands. Doing, not hearing, is what makes the difference with God.
ROMANS 2:13 MSG

Hard Times

Father, at times I feel like the hard times will never end, that all my time is spent trying to keep my head above water. In those times, help me to pray first and then reach out to help others who are having worse times than mine. Keep my eyes on You.

Don't burn out; keep yourselves fueled and aflame. Be alert servants of the Master, cheerfully expectant. Don't quit in hard times; pray all the harder. Help needy Christians; be inventive in hospitality.
ROMANS 12:11–13 MSG

Precious Time

Oh, how easy it is to fall into the trap of arguing with those who are godless or who, in essence, worship themselves, Lord. It's a waste of time that would be better spent studying Your Word and Jesus' life so that my life reflects Your glory.

Do not waste time arguing over godless ideas and old wives' tales. Instead, train yourself to be godly.
1 TIMOTHY 4:7 NLT

Busywork

Father, I waste a lot of time doing peripheral tasks—busywork—before I get down to the real work You've given me to do. But You expose them as distractions from the enemy to keep me from being effective. Forgive me. Show me when I fall into this trap.

Don't waste your time on useless work, mere busywork, the barren pursuits of darkness. Expose these things for the sham they are.
EPHESIANS 5:11 MSG

Wise Time Management

Lord, every Christmas I say that this year I'll do better about wisely using each moment of time. Yet I find myself creating odd jobs that distract me from doing the most important work of proclaiming the reason we celebrate Christmas. This year, help me to stay "on task."

Walk in wisdom toward outsiders, making the best use of the time.
COLOSSIANS 4:5 ESV

Ceaseless Prayer

Father, one of Your instructions to believers is to pray without ceasing. I know that doesn't mean I have to stay on my knees, hands clasped together twenty-four hours a day. But through Your Spirit within me, I can stay in a mind-set of prayer, alert and persistent in prayer for all believers.

Pray in the Spirit at all times and on every occasion. Stay alert and be persistent in your prayers for all believers everywhere.
Ephesians 6:18 nlt

Time Is Short

Lord, we live in an evil world. Man's cruelty is astounding. Yet You sent Jesus into this evil place to pay the astronomical price for our sin. Help me to walk in Your wisdom and to make the best use of the short time to proclaim Your salvation to those who haven't heard.

Look carefully then how you walk, not as unwise but as wise, making the best use of the time, because the days are evil.
Ephesians 5:15–16 esv

Telling Time

Father, ever since You established time at the creation of the world, You have used it to teach us of Your infinite love, patience, and faithfulness. When the set time had fully come, You sent Your Son to pay our sin debt, once and for all, so that we could live in hope.

For whatever was written in earlier times was written
for our instruction, so that through perseverance and the
encouragement of the Scriptures we might have hope.
ROMANS 15:4 NASB

Live for Today

Father, You are teaching me that there is nothing I can do to change the past. It's already covered in the blood of Christ. Plus, Your blessings in Christ Jesus are so abundant in the present, it is difficult to brood over the past. So help me to live for You today.

God keeps such people so busy enjoying life
that they take no time to brood over the past.
ECCLESIASTES 5:20 NLT

My To-Do List

The almighty to-do list rules many of us, especially at Christmastime. More activity than usual crowds into our November and December calendars. Then an unexpected "must-do" event throws everything off. So we make lists, hoping that will keep us on task. But the truth is, the unexpected will mess up our lists, too. Soon we find ourselves running in circles, exhausted, short-tempered, and not very likeable. Proverbs 16:3 tells us to "commit to the LORD whatever you do, and he will establish your plans" (NIV). So this Christmas, put God in charge of your to-do list, and let Him order your days.

Enjoy Life

I like to work with a to-do list, Father. It's so satisfying when I can mark off completed tasks. But at Christmastime, my list seems to grow, not shrink, each day. Then I get uptight and my temper is shorter. Help me to complete each task—even the monotonous ones—with joy.

It is good for people to eat, drink, and enjoy their work under the sun during the short life God has given them, and to accept their lot in life. And it is a good thing to receive wealth from God and the good health to enjoy it. To enjoy your work and accept your lot in life—this is indeed a gift from God.
ECCLESIASTES 5:18–19 NLT

Confirm Our Work

Lord, one reason I like my to-do list is the satisfaction I have when I know I'm operating within the purpose You have ordained for me. I see it as one form of confirmation from You that I am on the right track. Thank You, for each confirmation You give.

Let the favor of the Lord our God be upon us; and confirm for us the work of our hands; yes, confirm the work of our hands.
PSALM 90:17 NASB

Honor God

Father, the longer my to-do list, the more I tend to fall behind, showing up late for work or for commitments I've made in other areas. I'm more focused on that list than I am in representing Jesus to a lost world. Show me how to be consistent no matter what.

Don't put it off; don't frustrate God's work by showing up late, throwing a question mark over everything we're doing. . . . People are watching us as we stay at our post, alertly, unswervingly. . .in hard times, tough times, bad times.
2 CORINTHIANS 6:3–4 MSG

Sleep Well

When my to-do list is long, I tend to forget who is in control, Lord. Things I want start to take precedence over what You desire. I can't sleep well, thinking of everything on the list that still needs doing. This Christmas, help me to make my to-do list with You.

People who work hard sleep well, whether they eat little or much. But the rich seldom get a good night's sleep.
ECCLESIASTES 5:12 NLT

Hard Work Profits

Father, when my to-do list is especially long at Christmas, it's a good reminder to know that all hard work leads to profit. There's no payoff for just talking about it.

All hard work brings a profit,
but mere talk leads only to poverty.
PROVERBS 14:23 NIV

Commit Your Work to God

At this busy time of year, Father, help me to commit each day, each task, to You. Then You will establish my plans according to Your will.

Commit your work to the LORD,
and your plans will be established.
PROVERBS 16:3 ESV

Work Hard

Father, we are not given a lot of time on earth—a mere blip in the light of eternity. So I need to make my life count, to order my to-do list with the work You would have me do, and to put all my energy into completing those tasks to Your glory.

Whatever your hand finds to do, do it with all your might,
for in the realm of the dead, where you are going, there is
neither working nor planning nor knowledge nor wisdom.
ECCLESIASTES 9:10 NIV

Honor the Hard Worker

Lord, I'm overwhelmed at the length of my to-do list, until I bring it before You to determine what it is You want of me. You have promised strength and honor for the ones who work to bring honor to You. Show me what You have planned for me to do today.

Honor her for all that her hands have done,
and let her works bring her praise at the city gate.
PROVERBS 31:31 NIV

Work with Integrity

Father, You want Your children to work with integrity, busy with the work You have each one to do. I know when my to-do list is long, I'm tempted to ignore it and give in to idleness. Help me to not grow weary of doing Your work.

Some among you walk in idleness, not busy at work, but busybodies.
Now such persons we command and encourage in the Lord Jesus
Christ to do their work quietly and to earn their own living.
As for you. . .do not grow weary in doing good.
2 THESSALONIANS 3:11–13 ESV

God Is My Boss

Lord, when I do the work You have called me to do, I feel Your pleasure. It's easy to forget when I work a "secular" job that You are my ultimate boss. So help me to remember; it's easier for me to accomplish my tasks with joy.

Whatever you do, do your work heartily,
as for the Lord rather than for men.
COLOSSIANS 3:23 NASB

God's Strength

Thank You, Lord, for the strength You give me for the work to which You've called me. I'm in awe that You consider me trustworthy. You knew what this work would entail, and You appointed me to serve You long ago, before the foundation of the world.

I thank Christ Jesus our Lord, who has given me strength to do his work. He considered me trustworthy and appointed me to serve him.
1 TIMOTHY 1:12 NLT

Time Is Limited

Father, my time on earth is limited. But I long to hear, *"Well done, My good and faithful servant"* when I arrive in heaven. So help me in the work You have given me. Give me knowledge and wisdom in the planning phase as well as in the execution.

Whatever you do, do well. For when you go to the grave, there will be no work or planning or knowledge or wisdom.
ECCLESIASTES 9:10 NLT

My Worries

Worry eats at us from the inside out, but it's still a universal problem. At Christmastime especially, stress levels soar, adding to the anxiety and leading to panic attacks. Most of us would do ourselves a favor if we would take a "chill pill." But God has already given us "chill pills" in His Word: Don't be anxious. Pray about everything, with thanksgiving. Throw your worries on God. He'll sustain You. He cares for You. Learn to put relaxing activities into your schedule. Take time to praise God for the gift of His Son. Rejoice in His salvation.

Anxious Looks

Father, I so easily get bogged down with anxiety, especially when I'm faced with impossible time limits or super-long to-do lists. Christmas is one of those times when I wonder if I will get everything on my list done. Remind me that Your strength and help are mine when I ask.

"Do not fear, for I am with you; do not anxiously look about you, for I am your God. I will strengthen you, surely I will help you, surely I will uphold you with My righteous right hand."
ISAIAH 41:10 NASB

Yesterday, Today, Tomorrow

Lord, worrying about yesterday is wasted since there's nothing I can do about it now. And worrying over tomorrow is also a waste of time since I don't know what it will bring. Help me to live today for You without worry, knowing You are in total control.

"So don't worry about tomorrow, for tomorrow will bring its own worries. Today's trouble is enough for today."
MATTHEW 6:34 NLT

Don't Fret

Father, sometimes I allow things, people, or activities to crowd out my prayer time. I get so busy I forget that You command me to always be in an attitude of prayer. Then worry settles in, and peace flees. This Christmas, help me to remember to pray about everything.

Don't fret or worry. Instead of worrying, pray. Let petitions and praises shape your worries into prayers, letting God know your concerns. Before you know it, a sense of God's wholeness, everything coming together for good, will come and settle you down. It's wonderful what happens when Christ displaces worry at the center of your life.
PHILIPPIANS 4:6–7 MSG

A Martha Complex

Christmas is a time that I tend to be most like Martha, Lord, "anxious and troubled about many things." Church programs, school concerts, holiday parties, and family get-togethers all combine to pull me away from much-needed time sitting at Your feet, soaking in Your presence. Show me how to be Mary.

But the Lord answered her, "Martha, Martha, you are anxious and troubled about many things."
LUKE 10:41 ESV

God's Love

Nothing in this world or the next can ever separate me from Your incomprehensible love, Father. No matter how hard the enemy tries to make me believe otherwise, all I have to do is remember You sent Jesus to die as the perfect—only—sacrifice for my sin. Amazing love.

And I am convinced that nothing can ever separate us from God's love. Neither death nor life, neither angels nor demons, neither our fears for today nor our worries about tomorrow— not even the powers of hell can separate us from God's love.
ROMANS 8:38 NLT

God Cares

Father, who better can I give my worries to than to someone who loves me as You do? The enemy tries to blind me to Your love, to cheat me of Your precious peace, in order to keep me defeated. For those battles, help me to keep my shield and sword ready.

Give all your worries and cares to God, for he cares about you.
1 PETER 5:7 NLT

Don't Be Afraid

How many times do I allow anxiety to rule my choices,
Lord? For every day in the year there is a different "fear
not" or "do not be afraid/anxious" statement in Your
Word. In every instance, You are beside me, encouraging
me, *"Be strong. I have this. Wait on Me."*

Say to those who have an anxious heart, "Be strong;
fear not! Behold, your God will come with vengeance,
with the recompense of God. He will come and save you."
ISAIAH 35:4 ESV

God's Rest

Father, I too often depend on work You never intended
for me in order to provide the basic necessities of life. I
end up anxious and exhausted. Help me to keep my ears
open to the Spirit's guidance, knowing You alone provide
my needs, including rest.

It is useless for you to work so hard from early morning
until late at night, anxiously working for food to eat;
for God gives rest to his loved ones.
PSALM 127:2 NLT

God Is with You

King David left Solomon a monumental task—
building Your temple, Father God. But David gave him
encouragement: "God is with you in every detail. Be
bold and courageous. Don't worry." When I get bogged
down in a task that is bigger than I am, help me to take
David's advice: "Don't worry."

David continued to address Solomon: "Take charge! Take heart!
Don't be anxious or get discouraged. GOD, my God, is with you in this;
he won't walk off and leave you in the lurch. He's at your side until
every last detail is completed for conducting the worship of GOD."
1 CHRONICLES 28:20 MSG

Anxiety Multiplication

Father, why is it that anxious thoughts multiply like
rabbits? When my worrying turns into a panic attack,
I know my only help is to bring my thoughts into line
with Philippians 4:8, my eyes firmly fixed on Jesus. Your
Word tames my anxiety and allows me to rest.

When my anxious thoughts multiply within me,
Your consolations delight my soul.
PSALM 94:19 NASB

Put Down Deep Roots

Father, You invite any who are anxious to seek You. You compare them to trees planted by a water source. There the roots go deep into the ground to connect with underground sources. Make me strong in the years of hardship and drought, and make my fruit plentiful.

"He is like a tree planted by water, that sends out its roots by the stream, and does not fear when heat comes, for its leaves remain green, and is not anxious in the year of drought, for it does not cease to bear fruit."
JEREMIAH 17:8 ESV

Public Speaking

The time before the Lord's return is short, Father. As the persecution of believers increases, one day soon I may have to speak before a court of law to make a defense for the Gospel. Calm my spirit when that happens, for You will put Your words in my mouth when I need them.

"When they deliver you over, do not be anxious how you are to speak or what you are to say, for what you are to say will be given to you in that hour."
MATTHEW 10:19 ESV

Relax, God Has This

Father God, help me to relax, knowing You have everything under control. Fretting shows others that I am clinging to my agenda, not resting in You.

"And you? Go about your business without fretting or worrying. Relax. When it's all over, you will be on your feet to receive your reward."
DANIEL 12:13 MSG

A Healthy Body

Father, worry causes so many physical problems, especially when I refuse to let it go. Help me to release this burden so I may live a whole and healthy life.

So refuse to worry, and keep your body healthy. But remember that youth, with a whole life before you, is meaningless.
ECCLESIASTES 11:10 NLT

Scripture Index

Celebrate Jesus' Birth with these great titles from Barbour Books!

Available wherever great Christian books are sold!